MW00810982

THE HISTORY OF

NFL FOOTBALL

FOR KIDS

Basic Knowledge of NFL Football
History With Some Fun Facts and Records

WILLIAM LAWSON

TABLE OF CONTENTS

INTRODUCTION

I grew up with football.

I grew up with the sights, the smells, the sweat, the tears, the blood, the wins, and the losses. I was practically born onto the field, finding an instant passion and love for the sport since I could barely open my eyes.

I did not grow up with hockey.

I remember each Thanksgiving that my family would get together and watch a hockey game. Whether I was 4, 6, 8, or 10, the rules never got any easier for me to understand. While my family was there cheering on different players and aspects of the game I couldn't even see, I felt uninterested, bored, and probably drank a little too much diet soda. In other words, it's never fun not knowing what is going on in something when everybody else is so into it.

That's the thing about football here in America: Fans are *very* into it. From crazy outfits to dramatic face paint, to screaming at the top of their lungs for three hours straight, one thing is clear: Americans love their football.

My goal for all of you in this book is to be able to get to a place of basic football knowledge and enjoyment.

(Courtesy of unsplash.com.)

If you're someone who has never watched football nor any other type of sport growing up, there are a few things you need to pick up while watching your first football game. You need to understand that: A) Other players try to crush the player with the ball, B) The yellow flags thrown by the "zebra guys" mean that a player on the field did something wrong, and C) If you get the ball into the "end zone" that results in 6 points.

But what about a field goal? How come in a game where big, scary men are trying to crush smaller, slightly less scary men, do the teams sometimes trot out a tiny kicker to try and kick the ball through yellow uprights? How many points is that? Why would a team do that? When would a team do that?

What about the coaches? What do they do? Who are they talking to when they are shouting into their headsets? How come they get a red flag instead of a yellow one and how come they rarely ever throw it? Don't even get me started about punts.

The moral of this mini-rant is that the basics of football are quite clear—tackle the player with the ball, score points, beat your opponent—there are so many little tidbits that go into fully understanding the game.

The most beautiful part of the sport? I have been watching football literally for decades and I am still sometimes confused by something that happens on the field. There are so many rules, regulations, and scenarios possible that truly learning *everything* there is to learn about the game is nearly impossible.

Don't worry, though, as we won't be going that in-depth in this book.

My goal for the book, above all else, is to give you a better knowledge, understanding, and appreciation of this wholly American game. While sports like basketball, hockey, and baseball are all popular too in this country, no sport better embodies the United States than some smash-mouth football.

In the book, I will go briefly into football history, some players, and some incredible teams we have watched throughout history. Also, I will be teaching you the fundamental rules of the game, what needs to be learned for you to enjoy a game instead of falling asleep, and some records and fun facts to keep the book interesting and engaging throughout.

More than anything else, like football, I want this book to be *fun*. Even if you are a football hater, you have taken the first step in reversing that thought process by purchasing this book.

If you keep an open mind about learning more about the game and come into this experience with an eagerness to learn and be wowed, I promise you this book will prove to be a useful resource.

If, instead, you approach it with hesitancy and a bias that you are not going to find any of this interesting, then I have this to tell you: "Personal foul, unnecessary roughness, defense, number...you! A 15-yard penalty, automatic first down."

If none of that made sense, then congratulations! You have come to the right place.

Strap on your helmets, shove in your mouthguard, pad up, and prepare for a lot of heavy contact...this is about to get *fun*.

CHAPTER 1

WHAT IS
AMERICAN FOOTBALL?

The answer can be the very first lesson we learn in this journey together. You may be asking, how come I made sure to add 'American' before football? First off, good question! Second off, there are two reasons why I did this. First, 'football' as it is known in other parts of the world—namely Europe—is our soccer! That's right, if you head over to Germany and start saying "football this" and "football that," the great folks of Germany will likely think you are talking about soccer. To clarify, there are two other famous football leagues across the globe: the Canadian Football League (CFL) and the Australian Football League (AFL). These two leagues have vastly different rules than our league, the National Football League (NFL), and that could be good material for a second or third book. Important to remember: This book focuses only on the NFL!

(Courtesy of unsplash.com.)

With that out of the way, let's get into what this chapter is going to be about. Unfortunately, you can't jump directly into the fun without first learning a little bit about the basics. In this chapter, we will learn a little bit about how football was created and how it has changed throughout the years. This change mainly focuses on things such as league changes, uniforms, and player safety.

It's important to learn the basics of the sport so we can better understand a few definitions and terms as we continue to increase our knowledge of this great game!

How and When Football Was Created?

When you think of all the odd rules, regulations, and ideas that go into the average football game, it starts to beg the question: "Who came up with all of this stuff?" For this, we have to go back to November 12, 1892, more than 120 years ago! This was the day on which the Allegheny Athletic Association football team beat the Pittsburgh Athletic Club. Though none of this was all that important, football had been played before this, this occasion was the first time a football player— William 'Pudge' Heffelfinger—was paid to play the game. He was paid $500, an amount that equals out to just over $15,000 by today's standards. Not bad for one game, Mr. Pudge!

To the surprise of very few, football was spawned by creating two popular sports of the time, rugby and soccer, into one joyous game. The first football game ever played was between Rutgers and Princeton in 1869. It wasn't until the 1880s, however, that rule changes took a largely wild game and started to turn it into the football that we know and love. The creator of these rule changes was Walter Camp, a rugby player from Yale.

"By the 1880s, most athletic clubs had a football team" (ProFootballHallofFame, n.d.). Not surprisingly, college athletes very much took to the competitive aspect of football, and games were highly competitive and oftentimes broke out into fights! Being a contact sport, it was a way for college kids to get out their aggression after a long day of classes.

This all helped set the stage for the infamous Allegheny Athletic Association vs. Pittsburgh Athletic Club showdown (AAA vs. PAC). Both clubs were looking for a competitive edge in what was quickly becoming a heated rivalry. It was the PAC, however, that eventually paid Pudge to join their squad, a move that officially made Pudge the first-ever professional player.

After the game, the two teams continued to scout the area for better players to help up their chances of beating their rival the next time an opportunity came around. The PAC scouted Chicago and quickly returned to Pennsylvania for another matchup with the AAA. In this matchup, the PAC chose to pay both Pudge and Knowlton 'Snakes' Ames of the Chicago team to play for the PAC in its upcoming game against the AAA.

The AAA, however, did not take the move lightly. "Thus alerted, the AAA did some scouting of its own and found that Ben 'Sport' Donnelly, a star end, and

Ed Malley would play with the AAA…" (n.d.). Thus, both the PAC and AAA had a little "extra ammunition" for their next contest.

Oddly enough, the game resulted in only one score by Pudge to result in a final 4-0 score. If that sounds like a weird score to you, then awesome! Back in 1892, touchdowns only counted for four points and not six points like they do today. After you score a touchdown (cross the ball into the opponent's end zone), you are allowed to kick an extra point (field goal) worth one point or "go for 2," which means to line up near your opponent's goal line and try to score again for an extra two points. Important note on the two-point conversion: If it fails, you are not awarded the one point you would have gotten for a field goal. In this situation, a little risk/reward is going on!

Funny enough, the classic game between the AAA and PAC resulted in a net profit of $621 for the AAA, which is over $16,000 by today's standards! Even though the game itself was low-scoring and slow, it still showed that, even early on, there was a ton of money to be had in football, both for the players and the owners!

Who Invented It?

Unlike the games of basketball and baseball for which there is one clear creator, the history of American football is slightly more muddled. While some date the origin of it back to the 1820s, others claim the sport wasn't made official until the "Pioneer Period" of 1869–1875.

Most historians and football fanatics will agree that the Pioneer Period bred the true origins of American football as we know and love it today.

As I already stated, the first football game known to have been played was between Rutgers University and Princeton University on November 6, 1869. The game was played at Rutgers field with two teams of 25 players each that attempted to score by kicking the ball into their opponent's field goal. Carrying or throwing the ball was not allowed! Rutgers won that game by the score of 6-4. Not quite the exhilarating 42-39 games we are used to seeing by modern standards, but certainly exciting for all of the fans in attendance. The game was still physical, brutal, and led to more than a little blood being spilled.

This game started a "football craze" across the country, with more and more teams picking up the sport as it grew in popularity. By 1873, most colleges in the country had some version of football being played in front of fans.

This helped open the door for Walter Camp, widely regarded as the "Father of American Football" (Wikipedia, n.d.). Camp, both a player and rules visionary, was the one who first proposed, in 1880, to drop the number of players on either side from 15 (it had dropped from 25 to 15 a few years prior) to 11. While this proposal was rejected at first, this rule change eventually passed in the late 1880. Even today, 11 is the number Walter Camp proposed 141 years ago (and counting)!

Camp's most famous change, however, was another rule that has stood the test of time. "...the establishment of the line of scrimmage and the snap from center to the quarterback, was also passed in 1880." Let me help break down those four terms quickly, as all of them can be confusing for people new to the game.

Line of Scrimmage: This is where the ball starts on a team's possession. Following the kick-off, this is where the ball is placed for the team to begin trying to march down the field and score. Each time a team completes a pass or runs the football forward (or backward!), this moves where the line of scrimmage is for the next play.

Snap: No, this is not a Thanos snap! The snap is the action of the ball being given to the quarterback by the center. It starts most plays. No player on either team can cross the line of scrimmage until the ball is snapped.

Center: The center is the player on the offensive side of the ball who snaps the ball to the quarterback. He is the middle player out of the five linemen. Offensive linemen are considered some of the biggest players in football, and it's their job to protect the quarterback.

Quarterback: When you think football, you are likely thinking of a quarterback. Tom Brady, Aaron Rodgers, Peyton Manning, Joe Montana, Joe Namath—all quarterbacks! The quarterback is the player who receives the snap from the center and decides (with defenders rushing at him!) what he's going to do with it. He can give the ball to the running back, a player designed to—you guessed it—run up the field or he can run it himself or pass it to one of his players.

We will learn a lot more about all of these terms coming up, but I hope this helped make the quote a little easier to understand.

Still looking back, our friend Walter Camp wasn't done revolutionizing the game. Though his original plan was to implement the line of scrimmage rules to increase activity and make the game more exciting, he quickly realized that teams, Princeton, in particular, were using their players' new skills to hold on to the ball for extended periods and draw the game out. In other words, his plan backfired! He then, in 1882, implemented the down and distance rule that required teams to go at least five yards in three plays or they had to turn the ball over to the other team. This rule expanded through time and is currently used in modern American football to the tune of four plays for at least 10 yards.

Some of the other rules added by Camp included being able to tackle a player below the waist, referees, scoring rules, and halves. All of these rules to some extent are still being used in the game today.

(Courtesy of unsplash.com.)

Camp retired from football in 1882 but stayed on as a fixture at rule meetings until he died in 1925. "The Walter Camp Football Foundation continues to select All-American teams in his honor" (n.d.).

A true revolutionary for the sport, Walter Camp and his various rule changes helped set the stage for the football that we know and love today. He is the true inventor of American Football and is considered to be one of the most important figures in football history (despite only playing for a few years).

But while his rule changes were considered revolutionary at the time, those rules would go on to change through the years as football became more and more evolved. In this next section, we will take a look at how rules have changed from the 19th century and how they continue to change today.

How Football Has Changed Through the Years

Games, like people, change and evolve through time. While some rules of old football made sense for the period, rules are ever-changing to help achieve the needs of fans, safety officials, and players.

The NFL now has a Competition Committee to change rules and update the game wherever they see fit.

While rule changes are implemented relatively quickly today to improve the safety of the players, this was not the case when the NFL was founded in 1920.

Back then, if a rule was to be changed, it could take literally years or decades for that change to go through. Today, rules can be changed from year to year!

One of the first big changes to be implemented by the NFL came as a result of the first-ever NFL playoff game in 1932. The game was being played between the Chicago Bears and the Portsmouth Spartans. "In that game, Chicago Bears fullback and future Hall of Famer Bronko Nagurski faked a plunge, stepped back, jumped, and completed a lob pass to Red Grange for a key touchdown in his team's 9-0 victory" (NFL, n.d.).

At the time of the game, the quarterback (or whoever had the ball) was not allowed to throw the ball from anywhere more than 5 yards behind scrimmage. In other words, the ball handler had to be at least 5 yards behind the line of scrimmage to throw a pass. In 1933, due in part to the outrage that Portsmouth showed after this game, the league changed the rule so a player could throw the ball from anywhere behind the line of scrimmage. That rule is still the same today.

Since early on, the NFL has claimed that it changes rules for the number one purpose of making the game more fun and entertaining for its fans. Hugh 'Shorty' Ray, an NFL Hall of Famer due to his changes to the rules of the game, "...crunched the numbers and found a direct correlation between scoring and higher attendance" (n.d.). Thus, the league began implementing rules that would raise the offensive entertainment value of the game, something that the fans met with open arms.

For the next 30 or so years, the league began to cool it on the changes and fell into a sort of lull as teams began focusing more on running the football than passing the football. This led to shorter games, less exciting plays, and many bored fans.

In 1974, the NFL implemented a package meant to bring excitement back into the game. Among these new rules were:

- ➲ Moving the goalposts back 10 yards, making kicks harder.
- ➲ Making all field goals missed beyond the 20-yard line result in an immediate turnover, meaning the other team got the ball at where the kick was missed.
- ➲ Moving kickoffs from the 40-yard line to the 35-yard line, resulting in more high-contact plays.
- ➲ Reducing penalties on offensive plays.

All of these rules, plus a few more, were meant to add more excitement and high-intensity action to the sport.

The result? A spike in passing yards per game and dip in running yards per game. Though running the football remains a fundamental aspect of the sport that teams still do in today's game, the league has certainly focused on more of a pass-happy league, much to the delight of fans! A 30-yard pass down the field is much more exciting than a 5-yard run.

Now, not all the rules were meant to give the game more entertainment. A little later down the line, the league put limitations on the "chop block," a highly dangerous play in which two offensive players rush down the field and block the same defensive player— one high and one low—resulting in many knee injuries for defensive players. The chop block, in the modern NFL, is a 15-yard penalty, meaning the team that committed the penalty needs to move back 15 yards before its next play!

Regardless of your stance on the NFL as a league, it's impressive to see them try out and implement new rules, something that other leagues like the (Major League Baseball (MLB), National Basketball Association (NBA), and National Hockey League (NHL) sometimes struggle with.

How the Uniforms Have Changed and Why

Back when football began in the late 19th century, there was hardly a uniform to speak of. Players were not wearing helmets, wore ragged shirts, and had very little padding. As the sport advanced, the uniforms have evolved. With the modern technology we have available, we are better able to diagnose concussions and head injuries and to create incredibly elaborate helmets to help keep the players safe.

The Helmet

The first time a helmet was implemented in a football game was an 1893 clash between Army and Navy. People had started to take note of how dangerous the game could be for potential head and neck injuries, so some players thought to bring helmets into the equation. It wasn't until 1939, however, that helmets became a requirement for football teams across the country.

"The first helmets used in football were made out of leather straps or mole skin fused together to protect players who had a concern for their own safety" (Daughters, 2013). These crude designs did little to help players avoid injury, so they gave way to the "ear flap/aviator models" down the line.

In the 1930s and 40s, the first plastic helmet was implemented by Illinois coach Robert Zuppke. Though the plastic helmet had some early drawbacks, things like price and demand, they eventually powered through and put the leather helmets of old out of business.

From there, players and teams began to paint logos on their helmets to show their school pride. These helmets were usually brightly colored and sported cool mascots and logos for extra style points!

Beyond that usage, however, the bright helmets could also make it easier for the quarterback to spot his receivers downfield. Receivers are players who run down the field to try and get open to complete a pass. With their brightly colored helmets, the quarterback could more easily spot his team's colors vs. the opponent's.

In the early 1970s, Riddell set the standard once again by introducing its HA series of helmets that featured vinyl pads inside the helmet that could be filled with air to further absorb impact and facilitate a more custom fit (2013).

Riddell has since been the premier helmet supplier and works closely with scientists to ensure players' safety and comfort are being protected in their helmets.

Though safety is number one, having the helmets be at least somewhat comfortable is also a nice luxury to have!

The Facemask

It is much harder to nail down the origins of the facemask. Considering football was originally played between young college kids who were looking to blow off a little steam, it should be no surprise that punches and jabs were thrown at faces during almost every game. This resulted in some players creating nose guards or other medieval-looking devices to keep their faces safe.

It wasn't until 1953 that Riddell made a facemask specifically for the Cleveland Browns' quarterback Otto Graham. It certainly wasn't the first facemask in football, but nailing down the true specific first facemask is almost an impossible task!

(Courtesy of unsplash.com.)

Unfortunately for Graham, his facemask was made with a Lucite shield. While smart on paper, the Lucite had a bad habit of smashing on impact, a flaw that would later get it banned from the NFL.

This led to Riddell implementing a BT-5 helmet with a built-in single-bar facemask, opening a floodgate that would later lead to double-bar, triple-bar, and all sorts of custom masks that you see in the NFL today.

Much like for its helmets, Riddell works closely with scientists to create the safest facemask designs for maximum player safety.

The Shoulder Pads

Oddly enough, the idea of protecting the upper body in football outdates the thoughts on protecting the head. The invention of shoulder pads came from L.P. Smock in 1877. Smock was a Princeton student at the time. The first shoulder pads were made out of leather and wool and sewed into jerseys.

It wasn't until the 1960s and 1970s that shoulder pads caught up to the helmets of the time. Switching from leather to plastic allowed the pads to be leaner and tougher for more durability.

As the materials changed, so did where the shoulder pads were being used to cover. Originally padding for just the shoulders, the plastic pads started to creep down the body and cover things like the ribs and upper chest.

Visually speaking, the change in shoulder pads to the beginning of the 20th century may be the most shocking of any equipment change. What started as a basic way to protect the shoulders turned players' frontside into a practical cocoon.

The efficient padding also allowed players to look sleek and quick as compared to the burly pads in the 1990s. Though it may not seem important to you and me, sleek padding and looking cool on the field is important to players as they have a lot of eyes on them.

The improvements made to new pads are "...more than skin deep, as the advancements also mean better ventilation, enhanced mobility, increased comfort and better protection" (2013).

The Pants

Compared to the helmet and shoulder pads, the pants haven't changed much since football's inception in the late 19th century. Padded football pants became a part of the game much earlier than the helmet and facemask and were worn by most players as early as the late 1880s.

Much like the shoulder pads, the early football pants had canvas and pads sewn into the pants themselves. After that, evolution worked its way up until eventually hip pads were implemented too.

Much like all of the other gear we have talked about to this point, the gear has become lighter, sleeker, and cooler for modern-day players.

Focusing on things like nylon and other synthetic materials, the goal of the pants is to be highly comfortable yet almost invisible.

The Shoes

Shoes are known as cleats now. It's quite incredible that early college football players were able to move the way they could with the boot-like devices they wore! The shoes were slow, clunky, and awkward.

Oddly enough, it was not the rise in technology that spawned upgraded shoes for the players like some of the other bits of gear we have seen so far. No, instead, it was implemented, in part, by the fans wanting more competitive action. Better athletic shoes would mean better traction and more incredible plays happening on the football field.

Another factor in making this decision was the fact that players had to plan in all sorts of weather conditions. While the boots worked fine on a sunny day, for instance, things would get much harder once it was raining or snowing. These combined factors helped spawn the cleats.

Taking notes from professional baseball and European soccer, cleats began when players attached metal onto their boots, giving themselves better traction in the icy weather.

From there, creators got rid of the boot design entirely and opted for the lower, sleeker, more advanced cleats.

The Ball

You can't have football without...well...the football! It is no surprise to anyone who knows anything about rugby that the rugby ball and American football are close in comparison. The rugby ball is the same shape, but slightly larger and made out of different materials.

This wasn't always the case, however. The first ball used in the inaugural game between Rutgers and Princeton in 1869 used a disgusting hybrid between a rugby ball and a soft basketball. The ball wouldn't hold its shape and was quite difficult to throw, kick, or even hold!

The leather football originated in 1887 from Spalding, better known at the time for creating baseballs than footballs. Though still awkward and blunt on both sides, it was much closer to the sleek football we know today than the ball used in the Rutgers vs. Princeton game.

"Over time the football's pointed ends became more pronounced and the body more streamlined by simple evolution and necessity rather than a dictated ruling" (2013). In other words, like all aspects of football, the ball evolved.

An interesting, lesser-known fact about the ball is that up until 1956 teams used a white football for night games, making it easier to see it in the dark. While it was eventually switched out for a brown football with white stripes, there is another interesting fact that comes with this idea: While the NFL eventually dropped the white stripes from its football, college football did not. To this day, college football teams use a brown ball with white stripes while the NFL's ball is all brown.

The 32 NFL Teams

Now, we get to the fun history. In today's NFL landscape, there are 32 teams stretching across the entire country, from Los Angeles to New York City. In this next section, I will briefly go through all 32 teams, how they got their famous name, and when the team was originally founded.

1921: Green Bay Packers

The Green Bay Packers, the first NFL team, was named after their original sponsor, the Indian Packing

Company. No, these folks were not movers. "Packers" referred to meatpacking, a popular profession around that area at the time.

Widely considered one of the most successful franchises in NFL history, the Green Bay Packers won the first-ever two Super Bowls under legendary coach Vince Lombardi.

1922: Chicago Bears

One year later, the Chicago Bears were formed. When looking at the Chicago Bears' name, one needs to remember that, at this time, baseball was much bigger in the United States than football. As a result, the team chose the name Bears because it was closely related to another Chicago team, the Cubs.

By picking the name in close relation to an MLB team, the owner at the time was doing his best to grab some of the fans of the Cubs and convert them to Bears fans.

Another quick note, Bears was also picked as the team's name because the owner believed NFL fans, on average, were bigger than baseball players.

1925: New York Giants

It took another three years for another team to join the fray. This time, it was a team from the Big Apple.

Following the same route as the Chicago Bears, the New York Giants tried to steal the name of an MLB team, as well. They succeeded, directly taking the Giants from the MLB and adding it as their official title.

More than this, the Giants also signified the many skyscrapers across New York City. The name made sense on both parts.

1925: Arizona Cardinals

Though it would take many years for the current Arizona Cardinals to make it to Arizona, the team was originally founded in 1920 but didn't settle into St. Louis, at the time, until 1925. The name came from their jersey color ...a cardinal red, and had nothing to do with the birds!

1933: Philadelphia Eagles

(Courtesy of unsplash.com.)

29

Known in the football world to be one of the most passionate and energetic fanbases, the Philadelphia Eagles fans love their Eagles, love the city, and love the green and white! Eagles games are almost always loud, rowdy, and energetic, though they aren't always kid-friendly!

There was then a long hiatus of close to a decade before another team joined the fold: The Philadelphia Eagles were another team named after a bird but having nothing to do with the bird. The team was named to pay homage to President Franklin D. Roosevelt's National Recovery Act of 1933. Though they would eventually become competitive, the Eagles struggled for many years after their formation.

1933: Washington Redskins

The now-defunct Redskins, who are now known simply as The Washington Football Team due, in part, to the racist backstory of the mascot, came about when their owner wanted to connect to the Native American people around the area. That being said, however, he also wanted to differentiate his team from the nearby Boston Braves. Thus, the name Washington Redskins was settled on. Washington is the first and only team, so far, to lose its original mascot due to racist undertones.

1934: Detroit Lions

A much more mundane origin story, the Detroit Lions wanted to be close in comparison to their MLB team, the Detroit Tigers. Moreover, they also wanted to be the true monarch of the league, much like the lion is the monarch of the jungle.

In an ironic twist, Detroit is one of the few teams in NFL history to never win a championship.

Though their goal was to create a monarch, that goal is a goal that they are still working towards!

1937: Los Angeles Rams

After another three years, another team was added. This time, it was the Rams. In quite possibly the most boring origin story of any of the NFL teams, owner Buzz Wetzel chose the name Rams because his favorite college team was the Fordham Rams. In essence, he simply stole the name from the school!

1940: Pittsburgh Steelers

In 1940, the Pittsburgh organization had the awesome idea to let Pittsburgh natives select the name for their team. In the first-ever effective name-that-team contest—an idea that would be stolen by many other teams—it was a steelworker from Pittsburgh who submitted the name Steelers. Working well with the rough and tough nature of the city, the Steelers' name stuck!

1945: Cleveland Browns

Another team that maybe lacked a little bit of originality when choosing its name, the Cleveland Browns were named the Browns to honor General Manager/Coach Paul Brown. A quick reference here: The general manager is the supervisor of the team and looks after things such as trading of players, coaching, and drafting players. The coach runs the team when it plays games by calling plays, talking to his team, and using strategies to help his team win. Paul Brown played both of these roles for the Cleveland football team, and thus they honored him by creating the Browns. For whatever reason, the mascot for this team is not a person, but a dog!

1950: San Francisco 49ers

This one likely doesn't need a rocket scientist to figure it out! Considering the gold rush of 1849 took place partly in California, it seemed only right for the San Francisco football team to honor that by calling themselves the 49ers. Another interesting fact: The 49ers are the only team in the NFL that have a number as a part of their name.

1953: Indianapolis Colts

Though the Colts have jumped around locations more than any other team, it seems, they have finally settled down in Indianapolis after a couple of stays in Baltimore (who would later adopt the Ravens). The Colts were called the Colts because Indianapolis is well-known for horse breeding, especially in the area closest to the stadium. This, mixed with the natural choice of a mascot being something fearsome like a horse made the Colt an obvious and popular decision.

1960: Dallas Cowboys

Though they are America's team, the Dallas Cowboys came onto the scene relatively late. The Cowboys chose this nickname because they wanted a slice of Texas culture. What screams Texas more than a cowboy riding a stallion into battle? Very few things!

1960: Denver Broncos

Another team that benefited from a name-that-team competition was the Denver Broncos. Fitting for more reasons than one, the creators of the football team liked the Bronco because it possessed traits like toughness and grace on the field. More than that, the Denver area has always been known to have wild broncos living in the area. This was a perfect fit!

1960: Los Angeles Chargers

In 1960, the NFL had a big year! One of the new teams added this year was the now Los Angeles Chargers, a team that originally was stationed in San Diego. Another team benefitting from a name-that-team competition, the name Chargers was picked early on because the general manager of the time liked the idea of his team's name mimicking the 'Charge!' cry that was often heard in many sporting events. To this day, the battle cry is still used during the Chargers' games.

1960: Buffalo Bills

Another team named after a person, the Buffalo Bills honored Buffalo Bill Cody, an American soldier, buffalo hunter, and showman. Having just one other professional team in their city—the often-bad Buffalo Sabres of the NHL—the Buffalo Bills have one of the most passionate fan bases in the NFL.

1960: New England Patriots

Another team, another name-that-team competition, this time for the New England Patriots. Thanks to Tom Brady (we will learn more about the legendary quarterback later), the Patriots are tied with the Steelers for the most championships in NFL history (6). The name was originally chosen to help show respect and honor towards the defenders of the

United States bearing the same name during the Revolutionary War.

1960: Las Vegas Raiders

Another contest. This name was chosen because raiders are historically good fighters. Much like the Bills, the Raiders may not have any championships in their long history, but they do have one of the most passionate fan bases in the entire league. Fans will often dress as full Raiders in silver and black face paint. Having moved more than any other team in the NFL, Oakland still loves their Raiders, even though they now officially reside in Las Vegas.

1961: Minnesota Vikings

Burt Rose, the general manager at the time for the Vikings, chose the name because Vikings were a proud people with a will to win. At the time, the Minnesota Vikings were the only team to represent an entire state (Minnesota) and not a specific city.

1963: New York Jets

(Courtesy of unsplash.com.)

MetLife Stadium, the home of the New York Jets, is one of the most unique stadiums in the NFL simply because it houses not one but two NFL teams! On certain Sundays, it is the home of the New York Jets. On other Sundays, it is the home of the New York Giants! NFL schedules have to make sure that they don't double-shift the Jets and Giants or else one of them would be left without a place to play on Sunday!

Out of all of the teams in the NFL, the Jets may have the most interesting journey in getting that name. Originally, they wanted to be the New York Dodgers. The Los Angeles Dodgers, one of the most storied teams in MLB history, objected to the name and did not allow this to occur. They cycled through a few names after that but none of them stuck. Finally, they settled on the Jets for the simple reason that Shea Stadium in New York at the time was close to LaGuardia Airport. Out of all the reasons to choose a nickname, this one is likely the simplest but also the most honest!

1963: Kansas City Chiefs

It isn't exactly politically correct in this day in age, but the reason the Chiefs selected their name back in 1963 was for the simple fact that lots of Native Americans lived in the Kansas City area. Already seeing teams like the Washington Redskins and Cleveland Indians forced to change their name, teams like the Atlanta Braves (baseball) and Kansas City Chiefs may be forced into something similar in the upcoming years.

1966: Atlanta Falcons

Speaking of Atlanta, the Falcons came onto the scene in 1966. This was another name-that-team contest, with Falcons being chosen because they are powerful and distinguished hunters. A beautiful bird and unique mascot choice, the Falcons are one of my favorite mascots in the entire league.

1966: Miami Dolphins

Another unique and cool mascot, the Dolphins were chosen for Miami due to the animal being the "smartest and fastest creatures of the sea." Though the 'smartest' part of that definition is likely true, it is interesting to note that they aren't the fastest animal in the sea. Animals like killer whales, barracuda, swordfish, and sailfish can all move much quicker than the dolphin. That being said, the mascot was still an awesome choice!

1967: New Orleans Saints

Much like the Chargers' nickname, the New Orleans Saints were based on, you guessed it, the famous "When the Saints Come Marching In" song. Sung passionately by many folks of New Orleans during the Mardi Gras festival, it seemed an obvious choice to honor the classic tune by choosing a nickname that went along with it.

1968: Cincinnati Bengals

This one is straightforward: The Cincinnati Bengals of 1968 were named after a previous Bengals' organization in the same city that survived from 1937 to 1941.

1976: Tampa Bay Buccaneers

The Bucs named themselves after 17th-century pirates who raided the Florida coast. The name is one of the more popular ones in the NFL, and so is the massive pirate ship that fires real cannons after every Buccaneers score in their home stadium. If you happen to be in Tampa and check out a Bucs game, make sure to stay far away from that ship...it's been known to cause some jump scares!

1976: Seattle Seahawks

The Seattle Seahawks' nickname was chosen due to the birds being abundant in the Pacific Northwest. The seahawk is known for its aggressive nature. This connects with the fans as well. They are some of the loudest, most passionate, and most energetic fan bases in the entire league.

1995: Jacksonville Jaguars

One of the newest teams in the NFL, the Jacksonville Jaguars got their name because a zoo in the state housed a Jaguar. The more interesting part of this story is the original design of the Jaguars' helmet. Closely resembling the same logo that Jaguar uses for its luxury cars, the car company threatened to sue the Jacksonville Jaguars if they didn't alter their logo. The

Jacksonville Jaguars obliged, avoiding a potentially ugly situation with a massive corporation.

1995: Carolina Panthers

The Panthers wanted to stand out from the rest of their competition by choosing light-blue colors and choosing a mascot that is powerful, sleek, and strong. It hasn't won them a championship, but they have appeared in two Super Bowls in just their first 26 years. It may not seem like a lot, but that's not a bad start!

1996: Baltimore Ravens

Likely my favorite reason for choosing a nickname, the Baltimore football team went with the Ravens to honor Edgar Allen Poe's famous work of the same name. If this seems kind of random, it makes more sense once you realize that Poe was a Baltimore native. Sleek, good-looking, and dangerous, Baltimore's ravens are likely as dangerous and unpredictable as Poe himself!

1999: Tennessee Titans

The Tennessee club wanted to choose a team name that showed strength, courage, toughness, and consistency. Thus, the Titans were born. The owners and coaches have taken the name to heart, too. Throughout the years, the Titans have shown a consistent will to run the football hard and hit their opponents harder! They are the definition of a tough franchise.

2002: Houston Texans

The only team established in the 21st century, the Houston Texans chose this name because a focus group gave them three potential options: The Apollos, the Stallions, and the Texans. All good choices, but the Texans name was ultimately chosen.

CHAPTER 2

THE BASICS OF FOOTBALL

Now that you have learned a little bit more about the history of the game, the NFL, and the 32 teams that make up the league, it is now time to dive into the basic rules of the game.

Football is a much more complex sport than people believe. While on paper it looks to be just, see the ball, get the ball, there are many positions doing different things on the field, coaches making decisions on which plays to call, and referees making sure that everything runs smoothly.

In this chapter, we will learn more about the basics of football and how it is played; competing leagues that are trying to (and have tried) to challenge the NFL; and the various positions on the football field, rules, and movements throughout the field.

Basics of Football

If you've never watched football before, even the most basic elements can be seen as difficult to grasp when you are watching a game at full speed. By breaking down each element, my goal is to give you all the true basics of football without overwhelming anyone!

Basics

The purpose of the game, above all else, is to move the ball down the field (by either throwing or running) towards and ultimately into your opponent's end zone. The end zone is a 10-by-53-yard section of the field that the defensive players are trying to defend.

(Courtesy of unsplash.com.)

To score a touchdown—crossing the ball into the end zone, it must be done by either running with the ball past the goal line (the introduction to the end zone) or throwing the ball downfield to a teammate into the end zone. The specifics of touchdowns can get hard to understand—we will talk more about it later—but a player must catch the ball thrown by a teammate with two feet in the end zone for it to be counted as a touchdown. The referees deem if the player's feet were successfully in on a passing score.

Downs

Downs are the most fundamental, yet highly confusing, element of the American football game. The offensive team must attempt to move the ball down the field during a possession. The field is 100 yards long by about 53 yards wide.

Wherever the team starts with the ball, this is their initial line of scrimmage. We learned about this briefly in the first chapter, and this line marks where the ball starts (horizontally) across the entire field. Once the initial line of scrimmage is counted, the offense has four plays to move the ball 10 yards down the field. This line is called the first-down marker.

Once they go past the first-down marker in less than four plays, the whole system is restarted! There is a new line of scrimmage and the first-down marker is set 10 yards down the field. The team, once again, has four plays to reach the new marker.

An important note: If a first down is not gained by the offense on any play happening on first, second, or third down, this does not mean they need to go back to their *original* line of scrimmage! Each time a team gains yards, the line of scrimmage moves up to match where the play ended. If the play is shorter than the first-down marker, the play moves to second down and so on.

If the offensive team fails to make it past the first-down marker in four plays, the possession switches over to the other team. Of course, the team with the ball will usually try and kick a field goal or punt it before this. Kicking a field goal is worth 3 points and it is when an offensive team's kicker runs onto the field and kicks it through the uprights. A punt occurs when a team knows they are not going to reach the first-down marker and simply wants to give the ball to the other team. By punting, the offensive team can make the opposing team's starting field position much more challenging than if they were to go for it on fourth down and fail.

While most scoring occurs close to either team's end zone, a touchdown can be scored starting anywhere inbounds on the field. In other words, a player doesn't have to stop running once he reaches the first-down marker. He should try to score! A touchdown is worth 6 points and a field goal is worth 3 points.

Plays

Plays are the complicated actions happening on the field during any given down. Way back when, plays were usually quite simple and resulted in a player running the football forward for a couple of yards. Since then, the game has adapted, evolved, and changed into a pass-heavy league. This means there are more trick plays, more advanced plays, and more ways to move the ball down the field quickly on any given play.

The plays are usually called by either the head coach, the offensive coordinator, or the quarterback. We have already learned about the head coach and quarterback, and so the offensive coordinator is the coach who is specifically hired to help engineer the offense for the team.

While plays are usually more closely connected to offensive players, don't forget that the defense needs to call plays, too! These are usually called by players on the field, head coaches, or the defensive coordinators.

The offensive team gets 40 seconds to put the ball in play or kick a field goal. If the offensive team is unable to snap the ball in this period, they are given a penalty that moves them five yards backward. There is always a game clock that resets to 40 seconds after every play.

Timing

Unlike soccer, which is played in halves, American football is played in four quarters at 15 minutes apiece. Whenever there is an incomplete pass, the clock stops. The clock also stops when a player runs out of bounds with two or fewer minutes remaining in either the second or fourth quarter.

Each team gets three timeouts per half. Timeouts can be called by anyone on the field, but are usually deployed by the quarterback or head coach. These timeouts last 30 seconds and allow the players to take a quick break.

Halftime is 12 minutes long, usually, but is extended to 20 or 30 minutes for the championship games (for example, the Super Bowl). The Super Bowl halftime show involves a performance by a famous musician and is seen as more of a party than an actual halftime show about football!

Lastly, there is a 10-minute overtime period if the two teams are tied at the end of the fourth quarter. In the playoffs, this time is extended to 15 minutes.

In overtime, the two teams flip a coin to see who gets the ball first. Whichever team starts with the ball gets one full possession to go down the field and score a touchdown. If they either 1) don't score, 2) score a field goal, or 3) turn the ball over to the defense, the team that started on defense takes over.

If the team that starts with the ball turns it over to the defense who scores a touchdown in the same play, the game is over. If the first team to get the ball doesn't score a touchdown but scores a field goal, the defensive team has a chance to match that score or win the game with a touchdown. After the first possession, the team's alternate possessions until either team wins with any type of score.

Scoring

As mentioned, touchdowns are worth 6 points and field goals are worth 3 points. You score a touchdown by getting the ball into the opposing team's end zone. In American football, all scoring plays are reviewed by the referees to make sure it is a legal score. This involves looking to see if the ball crossed into the end zone or if a receiver had both feet down in the end zone with possession of the football. If all of these parameters are checked off, it is a touchdown!

The other three ways teams can score points are as follows:

Extra point: The extra point is attempted by the kicker following a touchdown and is worth—you guessed it—one point.

Two-point conversion: Instead of kicking the extra point following a score, the team can opt to go for two points. This going for two is a single play that starts from the opponent's two-yard line. If the team scores, they get 2 points, and if they are stopped, they get 0. They are not allowed to kick an extra point after a failed two-point conversion. One fun note: If the defense somehow intercepts or picks up a fumble from the team going for two, they can return it the length of the field and score 2 points themselves. This is one of the rarest plays in all of football, but it does occur.

The last way to score points is a safety. A safety occurs when a player has the ball in their team's end zone and is tackled by the defense. The defensive team gets 2 points and the football back after the following kickoff. This is another play that doesn't happen too often, but it is always exciting when it does.

Positions

The positions on a football team are hard to understand and even harder to master. I will do my best to explain each of the following positions to the best of my ability. First, let us take a look at the offense.

Quarterback: The quarterback is the player who receives the snap from the center and will also sometimes call plays for his team. He is the player who throws the football down the field and is arguably the most important player on the entire football team. The quarterback uses a headset built inside his helmet to communicate with his coach and offensive coordinator throughout the game.

(Courtesy of unsplash.com.)

50

Running Back(s): The running backs (full and half) have among the most grueling positions on the football field. The main runner on the offense, the full back, receives the hand-offs from the quarterback and does his best to make his way up the field without getting tackled. The half-back is another option for running plays. In the modern-day NFL, running backs are asked to help block and catch passes, too. Running backs are among the most often-injured positions in football because of the pounding they take from defenders.

Wide Receiver(s): There are usually one to three of these players on the field at a time. The wide receivers run routes to get open so the quarterback can throw them passes. These receivers are usually the fastest and tallest players on the field to improve their catch radius.

Tight End(s): The tight ends are another position that seems to be getting more and more popular in the modern-day NFL. Tight ends were previously mainly used to help the offensive linemen (we will get to them in a minute) block for the running backs and quarterbacks and little else. As the league has evolved, the tight ends are now being used much like wide receivers. Another position that takes a lot of abuse from defenders, tight ends have to be fast, strong, and tough to survive some of the hits they take.

Tackles: There are two of these players on the offensive line, the line that is quite literally created to help protect the quarterback from the defense. On every offense line, there is a left tackle and a right tackle. These tackles position themselves on the furthest parts of the offensive line (the outside two spots on either side) and usually have to block the opposing team's fastest and strongest players. Offensive linemen are asked to block for their offensive skill players (quarterbacks, running backs, wide receivers, tight ends) and rarely get to touch the ball themselves. It isn't a glorious position, but it is necessary to have a good offensive line for any football team to succeed.

Guards: Working towards the middle of the five-man offensive line, the guards are the ones on the insides of the left and right tackles, respectively. Much like the tackles, there is a left guard and right guard on every football team. Guards are usually asked to do a little more in the running game than the tackles, as teams usually like to run up the middle instead of running to the outside.

Center: Finally, we have the center. If the quarterback is the most important position for the offense, then the center is likely second. The center is asked to do a lot! He has to communicate with the quarterback to have a successful snap. The center also has to block the nose tackle on defense, usually the largest and baddest guy each defense has to offer. He also has to snap the ball quickly and get ready to block while also creating space for his running back and protecting his quarterback. It is a really hard position and requires the right mix of brawn and smarts!

Now, for the defensive players:

Safeties: Each team has two safeties who are the two players furthest away from the quarterback and thus are usually used to help defend passing plays. However, a defensive coordinator can also bring the safeties up to help defend against the run, as well. The safeties are the last line for the defense, and if an offensive player gets behind them, that likely means the ball-carrier is going straight to the end zone!

Cornerback(s): The cornerbacks' job is simple (in theory!). They are tasked with matching up against the opposing team's wide receivers. Everywhere a receiver goes, a cornerback follows. Every time a quarterback tries to pass a ball to one of his receivers, it is the cornerbacks' job to break up that pass, try and intercept (catch) the ball, or tackle the receiver once he catches it. They are also asked to help out with running backs when they break through the offensive line.

Linebacker(s): There are usually three of these guys on the field for any opposing defense. The linebackers are the second line of defense, right after a runner gets past the defensive line (who we will discuss in a moment). Linebackers have been called the "quarterbacks of the defense" since they are usually the ones who call or receive the plays from coaches and tell the rest of the defense what the play is. One of the hardest positions in football, the linebackers are tasked with tackling running backs, receivers, tight ends, and quarterbacks while also sometimes having to play the role of a cornerback, too, when a tight end goes out to catch a pass. Without good linebackers, a defense is likely not very good!

Defensive Ends: There are two of these on each football team: A right end and a left end. The defensive end's main job is to try and get to the quarterback and force him to make bad decisions. Defensive ends are usually fast, strong, and can hit hard! They are also tasked, on running plays, to contain the running backs and not allow them to get to the outside where there is usually a lot of running room.

Defensive Tackles: Finally, we get to the defensive tackles. These are not the same as offensive tackles, as they are on the inside of the defensive line (which is usually made up of four players instead of five). While the ends are on the end of the line, the tackles are in the middle. Defensive tackles are almost always literally monsters! They are big, strong, scary, and tasked with wrecking the offensive line to either sack the quarterback or get to the running back behind the line of scrimmage. They are quite literally bowling balls and can quickly destroy an offensive player if they aren't blocked.

Finally, the special teams!

Kicker: The kicker is tasked with kicking field goals and kickoffs. The kickoff is the first play that happens in the game and involves the kicker kicking the ball down the field and allowing the opposing team to return that kick up the field.

Punter: The punter, the final position that we will touch on in this short introduction to the positions, is the player who punts the ball when a team doesn't want to use their fourth-down attempt. The punter tries to put the team returning the ball in poor field position, meaning they have to go a lot of yards to try and score.

Other Leagues Competing with the NFL

Though the competition is less than fearsome, many leagues have tried over time to compete with the giant that is the NFL. Whether these be other leagues in the United States, leagues from other countries, or

55

anything else entirely, there have certainly been attempts to steal some of the viewership away from the NFL. In this section, we will take a look at some of the leagues that are closest to the NFL in stature.

The United States Football League (USFL, 1983–1986)

The USFL had a pretty good go at it back in the 1980s when they attempted to compete with the NFL. Former President Donald Trump even got in on the action by purchasing the short-lived New Jersey Generals. The USFL was able to grab a couple of former NFL players to spice up their competition with the NFL, but the league eventually folded in 1986.

XFL (1991–2001)

There has since been a second attempt to resurrect the XFL as recently as 2020, but the league folded before it even began in part due to COVID-19. The original XFL was founded by WWE spearhead Vince McMahon and tried to unseat the NFL by adding a rougher style of play to its games. It was "promoted as football with fewer rules and bigger hits...the league featured such gimmicks as scantily clad cheerleaders and nicknames on the back of player jerseys" (Barrabi, 2020).

The XFL was surprisingly popular at first, but quickly fell out of favor with the fans and ended up costing McMahon over $70 million.

United Football League (UFL, 2009-2012)

The UFL used players formerly from the NFL to compile four teams who directly challenged the NFL's rule by playing in the fall (the time when the NFL starts up). Doomed from the beginning due to poor competition and only four teams, the league lasted a surprising three seasons before crumbling in 2012.

Arena Football League (AFL, 1987–2008, 2010–2019)

The AFL is unlike the other leagues here because it was able to gather somewhat of a niche in its two different stints. More than that, it had some lasting power as well in both of its iterations. Played entirely indoors using a shorter field, narrower goalposts, and other tweaks to try and spawn more action-packed, faster play, the AFL got some big names and solid viewership throughout its two tenures. The league was able to get 19 franchises to play simultaneously during its peak, but it eventually collapsed in 2019 with just six franchises still playing.

Alliance of American Football (AAF, 2019)

The AAF is a sad story because the league had a lot of potential. Surviving just one season because of financial problems, the league had good early reviews based on the solid product on the field and the players. They were able to grab a few big names from college football and the NFL, resulting in competitive play and good attendance. Alas, the league was not destined to succeed, and it eventually folded before the first season even finished.

(Courtesy of unsplash.com.)

CHAPTER 3

THE TOP 20 FRANCHISES
IN NFL HISTORY

N ow that we have gotten through the muddy parts of learning the game and a little bit about positions, we can now launch into some of the more fun stuff. Starting off in this chapter, we will be looking at the top 26 franchises of NFL history and how dominant they've been. Now that you know the 32 teams and the history behind them, it should be very interesting to learn which ones have been the most dominant since the league began!

Top 26 Teams with the Most Championships

26. Seattle Seahawks: 1 Super Bowl Win

The Seattle Seahawks have one Super Bowl win in their 45 seasons of competition. This may seem like a poor percentage, but winning the Super Bowl in the NFL is challenging beyond all belief.

Seattle was able to win their only Super Bowl in 2013 when they bested the Denver Broncos. Led by young quarterback Russell Wilson, the Seahawks destroyed the Broncos, winning that game 43-8! It was never a competition, with the Seattle defense leading them to victory.

The 2013 Seattle Seahawks had an excellent secondary, meaning the players who are the last line of defense that we discussed earlier. This includes cornerbacks and safeties. Seattle leaned on their defense that year, nicknaming themselves the "Legion of Boom."

The Legion of Boom was dominant in the Super Bowl, forcing two Peyton Manning (quarterback for the Broncos) interceptions and forcing a safety, too.

Offensively, Russell Wilson was effective, throwing two touchdowns, while star running back Marshawn Lynch had a touchdown of his own.

Seattle has been a consistently good team since this Super Bowl win, but they have not won another one since.

25. Providence Steam Rollers: 1 NFL Title

For you keen-eyed viewers out there, you may have spotted the difference between the Seattle Seahawks and the Providence Steam Rollers. While the Seahawks have one Super Bowl win, the Steam Rollers have one NFL Title. The difference between these two? Well, before 1967, when the NFL officially merged with the American Football League (AFL) to form the modern-day NFL, the NFL was a separate entity. Thus, it wasn't until that year, 1967, that the Super Bowl was born when the two powerhouse leagues combined into one. Championships that occurred in the NFL before 1967 are still considered legit champions, and this is why the Providence Steam Rollers have an NFL Title but not a Super Bowl.

This specific Providence Steam Rollers team, the 1928 Providence squad, was so special that they made their way onto the "NFL Top 100" teams of all time, ranking 98th. Despite only playing seven seasons in the NFL, the Providence Steam Rollers will forever be remembered because of this amazing 1928 squad.

Led by Gus Sonnenberg at running back, the Steam Rollers went 8-1-2 (8 wins, 1 loss, 2 ties) during the 1928 season, thanks in part to a defense that only allowed 42 points all season! That is incredible! In the modern-day NFL, teams are lucky if they allow less than 42 points in two games!

There was no official championship game back before the Super Bowl, but the Steam Roller got their title based on their winning percentage, barely edging out the second-place Frankford Yellow Jackets.

24. New York Jets: 1 Super Bowl Win

The Jets have one Super Bowl win in 1968, just one season after the combined NFL was founded. This was a huge momentum change for the league, as it appeared after the first couple Super Bowls that the AFL teams that joined the merger were not ready to compete with NFL powerhouses such as the dominant Green Bay Packers. The Jets were the first former AFL team to win the Super Bowl, handling the Baltimore Colts 16-7 in the 1968 Super Bowl.

Led by "Broadway" Joe Namath at quarterback who famously guaranteed the Jets' victory before the big game, the Jets finished the 1968 season with a record of 11-3 in the regular season. The Jets took care of the Oakland Raiders in the semifinals before beating the heavily favored (and NFL mainstay) Baltimore Colts in the championship.

Before this game, there were some talks that the league wouldn't make it simply because the original

NFL teams were so dominant and the AFL mergers were, well, not! The Jets helped pave the way for the league to become the entertainment powerhouse that it is today.

23. New Orleans Saints: 1 Super Bowl Win

The Saints came marching in for a Super Bowl title back in 2009 when they were able to defeat the Indianapolis Colts by a score of 31-17. Facing off with one of the best quarterbacks in NFL history, Peyton Manning, few predicted that the Saints would have a chance in that game. Led by their great quarterback, the now-retired Drew Brees, the Saints were able to overcome the challenge and win their first Super Bowl title. Since then, they've been a consistently good team but have not been able to make it back to the big game.

The 2009 version of the Saints was an amazing offensive team, ranking first in the entire NFL in points per game. This was thanks mostly to Brees and wide receiver Marques Colston, who finished the season with over 1,000 receiving yards and had 9 touchdowns. For wide receivers, 1,000 yards is a strong milestone to shoot for when you are looking at a good season. The same can be said for running backs, although their yards are on the ground vs. through the air for receivers!

With a passionate fan base and a great team, the 2009 New Orleans Saints squad remains one of the most dominant in recent memory.

22. 1926 Frankford Yellow Jackets: 1 NFL Title

Another team that won its title before the AFL-NFL merger, the 1926 Frankford Yellow Jackets are considered to be an even better team than the 1928 Providence Steam Rollers. When the NFL released its Top 100 Teams of all time a few years back, the 1926 Frankford Yellow Jackets ranked 81st.

Based in the Frankford neighborhood of Philadelphia, the Yellow Jackets were led by Hall of Fame Coach Guy Chamberlain, who also played for the team. The Hall of Fame, I should mention quickly, is the honor that every person involved with an NFL team shoots for. It is an exclusive club based in Canton, Ohio where only the greatest players, coaches, GMs, and owners are allowed to be enshrined there. If you are in the Hall of Fame, chances are you did something incredible with your football career!

The Frankford Yellow Jackets were simply dominant, ranking first in the league in points scored per game and ranking second in points allowed per game. They went 14-1-2 (14 wins, 1 loss, 2 ties) and were the first team in NFL history to record 14 wins in a season, a feat that is still considered incredibly impressive by today's standards.

21. Tampa Bay Buccaneers: 2 Super Bowl Wins

The most recent team to win a Super Bowl, the Tampa Bay Buccaneers already have two in just 45 years, not bad considering how old the league is!

The first title for the Buccaneers came in 2002. This Buccaneers team did it the old-fashioned way, leading the way with their fearsome defense while doing enough offensively to win a lot of games. The team went 12-4 in the regular season and easily galloped past the Oakland Raiders in the Super Bowl by a score of 48-21. The 2002 Bucs didn't have much pressure on them in any of their three playoff games. They started the playoffs that year beating the San Francisco 49ers by a score of 31-6. After that, they destroyed the Eagles to the tune of 27-10. Finally, they demolished the Raiders in the big game. The defense was amazing, led by three great players in linebacker Derrick Brooks, defensive end Simeon Rice, and defensive tackle Warren Sapp. This was a scary team.

The next Bucs team to win the Super Bowl came 18 years later with the 2020 Tampa Bay Bucs defeating the Kansas City Chiefs by a lopsided score of 31-9. This team had a harder time in the playoffs, playing close games against the Washington Football Team (31-23), New Orleans Saints (30-20), and Green Bay Packers (31-26) before cruising to a win against the Chiefs in the big game. Led by Tom Brady, considered to be one of the best players in NFL history (more on him later!), the Bucs had a great balance of offense and defense to lead them to a Super Bowl title. Offensively, it was Tom Brady and wide receiver Mike Evans (1006 yards, 13 touchdowns) leading the way while the defense was incredibly well-rounded. With another good-looking team in 2021, the Tampa Bay Bucs are looking for title #3.

20. Kansas City Chiefs: 2 Super Bowl Wins

(Courtesy of unsplash.com.)

The Kansas City Chiefs in the modern-day NFL are known for a few things: high-powered offense, awesome tailgating, and passionate fans! Appearing in the last two Super Bowls (and winning one of them), the Chiefs are among the best teams in the current NFL landscape.

Another team to win two Super Bowl titles are the Kansas City Chiefs. The first title came back in 1969, back when the combined league was starting. A dominant team that went 11-3 during the regular season, the Chiefs overcame the Jets, Raiders, and Vikings to win its first-ever Super Bowl. Led by a solid offense and mean defense, the Chiefs were well-balanced and hard to stop on both sides of the football.

Fast forward to 2019 and you have a much different version of the Chiefs. Led by star quarterback Patrick Mahomes, the 2019 Chiefs are considered to be one of the best offensive teams in recent memory. Mahomes threw for over 4,000 yards with just 5 interceptions during the regular season and was even more majestic during the playoffs. Led by the killer receiving duo of wide receiver Tyreek Hill and tight end Travis Kelce, the Chiefs overwhelmed their opponents with impressive plays, a ton of points, and a brilliant offense. Though they would enter the Super Bowl the following season as the favorites, they would eventually lose to Tom Brady and the Buccaneers.

19. Miami Dolphins: 2 Super Bowl Wins

The 1972 Miami Dolphins may be the greatest team in NFL history. Going a perfect 17-0 (including the playoffs), the Dolphins led the league in most points scored and ranked last in points allowed. They simply dominated opponents, led by legendary Hall of Fame Coach Don Shula.

Offensively, they pounded teams into submission with a pair of incredible running backs: Mercury Morris and Larry Csonka. Both had over 1,000 yards rushing in this glorious season. The team didn't pass often and dominated teams defensively by pressuring opposing quarterbacks and stopping the run. The only team to ever go undefeated and win the Super Bowl, the 1972 Dolphins will always be considered one of the best to ever play.

It didn't take Miami long to win another one! The second Super Bowl came a year later, in 1973. Though they didn't go undefeated this season (they lost two games), they still plowed their way through the playoffs and earned a second straight Super Bowl trophy. The dominant defense stayed the same while they upgraded their quarterback to Bob Griese, who threw 17 touchdowns. Morris and Csonka were once again the focal points on offense.

The Dolphins have been a poor 21st-century team, to say it lightly, and continue to struggle this season.

18. Baltimore Ravens: 2 Super Bowl Wins

Despite only being around for just over two decades, the Baltimore Ravens have been a consistently awesome football team in that span. Preaching things like dominant defense and running the football, the Ravens are tough, scary, and intimidating.

Their first Super Bowl came in 2000 when they went 12-4. Though being hardly above average offensively, this Ravens defense was quite possibly the greatest defense we have seen so far in the 21st century. They were tough, they were mean, and they got after the offense! Led by linebacker Ray Lewis and safety Rod Woodson, this defense struck fear into the eyes of any quarterback who was staring them down. Offensively, running back Jamal Lewis led the way with over 1,300 yards rushing in that season.

The next Super Bowl came in 2012 under Head Coach John Harbaugh. A decent team in the regular season (10-6 record), these Ravens hit another gear in the playoffs, taking out powerhouses like the Denver Broncos, New England Patriots, and San Francisco

49ers (Super Bowl). Led by solid quarterback Joe Flacco and star running back Ray Rice, the Ravens once again leaned on a great defense to get them past some of the awesome offensive teams they had to overcome in the playoffs.

Consistent and tough, the Ravens are almost always playoff contenders and seem to be headed there once again this season.

17. Arizona Cardinals: 2 NFL Titles

It's been quite a while since the Arizona Cardinals have been competitive in the NFL. The team has two NFL titles dating back to 1925 and 1947. Though they have been around since the inception of the league in 1967, the team has rarely been competitive and has reached its only Super Bowl in the 2008 season.

The good news for Arizona fans? This year's rendition of the Cardinals currently has the best record in the NFL. Led by young phenom quarterback Kyler Murray and a pesky tough defense, could this be the year that the Cardinals finally return to the big game?

16. Las Vegas Raiders: 3 Super Bowl Wins

Now we get to the teams with three titles. The Raiders were dominant in the late 1970s and early 1980s, picking up titles in 1976, 1980, and 1983.

The 1977 Raiders got the party started under legendary Hall of Fame Coach John Madden. This edition of the Raiders lost only one game and overcame the Patriots, Steelers, and Vikings to win their first championship.

In 1980, it was Tom Flores leading the team this time. The Raiders went 11-5, destroying the Philadelphia Eagles in the championship game by a score of 27-10.

Finally, in 1983, it was once again Tom Flores leading his team to a 12-4 season and eventual Super Bowl title. A great offensive team, the team leaned on star running back Marcus Allen and receiver Todd Christensen to help them reach the big game. Once there, they trounced Washington by a score of 38-9 to win their third Super Bowl in just seven seasons. Truly, this was a dominant stretch.

The Raiders have had solid teams since then, but they have been unable to regain that thunder, returning to the Super Bowl just once in the 21st century.

15. Los Angeles Rams: 2 NFL Titles and 1 Super Bowl Win

The first team to have a combination of NFL titles and Super Bowls, the Rams are a storied and proud franchise whether playing in St. Louis or Los Angeles.

The NFL titles came in 1945 and 1951.

After a long time of decent play, the Rams returned to the big game in the 1999 season when they lined up against the Tennessee Titans. Playing as the St. Louis Rams, this team was solid on both offense and defense, ranking among the top five in both categories. Finishing the season with a great record of 13-3, the Rams had to battle in the first two rounds of the playoffs, facing tough competition against both the Minnesota Vikings and Tampa Bay Buccaneers. The tough times didn't stop there, either. Facing a feisty and hungry Tennessee Titans team in the Super Bowl, it was an absolute battle between two good teams. It came down to the final play, but the Rams pulled it off.

Led by one of the greatest quarterbacks of all time, Kurt Warner, star running back Marshall Faulk, and great receiver Isaac Bruce, the Rams were a tough team to stop on offense.

The Rams have kept that tradition of great offense moving along in their current rendition, consistently putting up a ton of points in the modern-day NFL. The team made it to the Super Bowl back in the 2018 season, but they eventually lost to Tom Brady and the New England Patriots. They are great once again this season.

14. Denver Broncos: 3 Super Bowl Wins

(Courtesy of unsplash.com.)

Playing in Denver, Colorado, has its perks. Besides being one of the most naturally gorgeous settings in the United States with 300 days of sunshine and stunning mountain views, Denver is also a mile high in the air (literally!). Though that doesn't seem like much to you or me, visiting teams need to get used to the altitude and will often have inhalers and extra air on the sidelines for the players struggling with the altitude.

Another proud franchise, the Broncos have three Super Bowl wins in the past 23 years...not a bad number whatsoever! Those Super Bowls came in the 1997 season, the 1998 season, and the 2015 season.

In 1997, it was the John Elway show. The quarterback of the Broncos threw for over 3,000 yards and had 27 touchdowns in that season. Paired with legendary Coach Mike Shanahan, the team sported the best offense in football. Elway, paired with Hall of Fame running back Terrell Davis and Hall of Fame tight end Shannon Sharpe, was simply impossible to stop for both the 1997 and 1998 seasons.

It would take Broncos fans another couple of years to win another title, but that eventual payoff came in 2015 with Hall of Fame quarterback Peyton Manning at the helm. It was not Manning's best statistical season, as he was facing numerous injuries and struggling at the end of his career. That being said, he did enough offensively to let his defense carry the Broncos to victory. The Broncos have fallen off since then, but folks in Denver are hoping for a return to glory sooner rather than later.

13. Canton Bulldogs: 3 NFL Titles

It's been a long time since we've seen the Canton Bulldogs in action, but they were an early titan in the NFL. Winning league championships in 1916, 1917, and 1919, that feat stands tall as one of the most dominant three -year stretches in NFL history.

Though the Bulldogs disbanded near a century ago, the legacy of Canton still lives on in the NFL. The Hall of Fame, which I have previously mentioned being a place where the best players, coaches, and GMs go to forever be enshrined in football history, is in Canton, Ohio.

12. Detroit Lions: 4 NFL Titles

Though they have been one of the weakest teams in the NFL since the merger, the Detroit Lions were a dominant NFL team way back when. Winning titles in 1935, 1952, 1953, and 1957, the Lions were riding high flying into the AFL-NFL merger. Unfortunately, it simply hasn't happened for the Detroit squad since then.

They have had a season in which they won zero games, haven't won a playoff game since 1991, and have only gone to the playoffs three times in the 21st century.

Unfortunately, it doesn't look like this season is going to go any better.

11. Philadelphia Eagles: 3 NFL Titles and 1 Super Bowl Win

The Eagles were solid in a stretch before the 1967 merger, winning a combined three titles in 1948, 1949, and 1960. Following that stretch, they were near-silent for over 50 years. Fear not, however, the Eagles won their first elusive Super Bowl following the 2017 season, a year in which they dominated their way to a 13-3 record. This was not a normal Super Bowl win for the Eagles, though. Throughout the regular season, star quarterback Carson Wentz played like one of the best players in the NFL. He had over 3,000 yards, 33 touchdowns, and just 7 interceptions. Right before the playoffs, however, he got injured and was forced to miss the entirety of the rest of the season. Fear not, however, as backup quarterback Nick Foles stepped into the starting role and guided the Eagles to their first-ever Super Bowl win.

Led by star tight end Zach Ertz offensively and a stingy defense, the Eagles were able to scrape past the Falcons in the first round of the playoffs, blow out the Vikings, and then eke out a win against Tom Brady and the Patriots in the Super Bowl.

It's been a mixed bag since then.

10. Cleveland Browns: 4 NFL Titles

The Browns may be the laughingstock of the current NFL, but there was a time, in the 1950s when the Browns were the top dogs. They won NFL titles in 1950, 1954, 1955, and 1964, just three years before the merger. Unfortunately for the Browns, 1964 would be the last time they even saw a chance at winning the championship. The Browns have made the playoffs just 15 times since the merger, with 12 of those happening before 1990.

While the Browns fans are as passionate as they come, their product on the field has oftentimes left a lot to be desired. The Browns had a chance to make a run for the Super Bowl last year but lost to the Chiefs in the second round of the playoffs.

9. Indianapolis Colts: 3 NFL Titles, 2 Super Bowl Wins

The Colts won three NFL titles as the Baltimore Colts in 1958, 1959, and 1968. They then followed up the victory in 1968 by winning one of the first-ever Super Bowls in 1971. In a special season in which they finished 11-2-1, the Colts were solid on both sides of the football. An elder Johnny Unitas was the quarterback for the team and though it wasn't his best statistical season, he still made big plays when necessary.

The next Super Bowl win wouldn't come until 2006 for one of the best offensive teams in NFL history. Though the defense was subpar, Hall of Fame Quarterback Peyton Manning and Hall of Fame Coach Tony Dungy led a fearsome offense to a 12-4 regular-season record before running over the Chiefs, Ravens, Patriots, and Colts on the way to a Super Bowl victory.

Manning was fantastic this season, throwing for over 4,000 yards and finishing with 31 touchdowns. Star receiving duo Marvin Harrison and Reggie Wayne were also near impossible to stop on defense.

While the Colts have been solid ever since then, they have yet to regain that edge to take them to the next level.

8. San Francisco 49ers: 5 Super Bowl Wins

(Courtesy of unsplash.com.)

The San Francisco 49ers have been one of the most dominant teams since the AFL-NFL merger of 1967. Winning an amazing five titles from 1982 to 1995, the team cemented a legacy of dominance with wins over other great franchises such as the Miami Dolphins and Denver Broncos.

The first ring came in 1981 when legendary Coach Bill Walsh was able to sneak past the Cincinnati Bengals by a score of 26-21. Led by star quarterback Joe Montana and receiver Eddie Clark, the 49ers were able to ride a dominant offense past a feisty Cincinnati squad. The defense, led by Ronnie Lott, was also as good as they come.

In 1983, the team was even better, posting a 15-1 record under Walsh and Montana. Getting help from running back Wendell Tyler, the 1983 49ers ran past the Miami Dolphins in the Super Bowl, earning them a second Super Bowl ring.

The next ring came in 1988. This time, Joe Montana teamed up with star running back Roger Craig and star wide receiver Jerry Rice to form one of the most dangerous threesomes in the entire league. The offense was unstoppable, and the 49ers once again snuck past the Bengals by a score of 20-16.

Ring four came a year later with roughly the same team, Joe Montana was awesome and Jerry Rice kept on improving.

The final ring came in 1994. Joe Montana had retired but was replaced by another star quarterback in Steve Young. Impressing with both his arm and his legs, Young was a star in the making. Of course, it helped to have a still dominant Jerry Rice.

The 49ers got back to the Super Bowl in 2019, but have struggled in the few seasons since.

7. Dallas Cowboys: 5 Super Bowl Wins

America's team, the Cowboys, were dominant in a stretch from 1993 to 1996. They won three titles in that span, adding to their previous two titles earned in 1972 and 1978.

The 1971 team, led by legendary coach Tom Landry and quarterback Roger Staubach, were the first Cowboys team to lock in a Super Bowl victory, defeating the Dolphins by a score of 24-3.

Their next Super Bowl, again under Tom Landry, came in 1978 with a 27-10 smashing of the Denver Broncos. A dominant offensive team again led by Staubach also had a 1,000-yard rusher in Tony Dorsett.

Following a brief period of subpar play, the Cowboys found themselves back on top in 1992, this time coached by Hall of Famer Jimmy Johnson. Finishing with a 13-3 record that season and being one of the best offensive teams in football, the Cowboys leaned on Hall of Famers quarterback Troy Aikman, running back Emmitt Smith, and receiver Michael Irvin. The three were almost impossible to stop, and this proved to be the case when the team demolished the Bills 52-17 in the Super Bowl.

The next title came the next year, with the team riding a 12-4 record to another Super Bowl win over the Bills, this time slightly more competitive at 30-13.

Their final Super Bowl came in 1995 when they overcame the Steelers by a score of 27-17. This was

Aikman, Smith, and Irvin's final Super Bowl win, a trio that would go down in history as one of the most dominant the sport has ever seen.

6. New England Patriots: 6 Super Bowl Wins

If the San Francisco 49ers were dominant, the New England Patriots were even better. Currently tied with the Pittsburgh Steelers for most Super Bowl wins with six, the Patriots have the incredible distinction of winning all six of those titles in the 21st century. A legendary duo of head coach Bill Belichick and quarterback Tom Brady will do that for you.

The Patriots own title wins over the Rams (2002 and 2019), Panthers (2004), Eagles (2005), Seahawks (2015), and the Falcons (2017). Tom Brady has the most individual championships of all time with seven (six with the Patriots and one with the Bucs).

What made the Patriots' domination so incredible to watch was that they could do it on both ends. Brady is undoubtedly one of the best offensive players of all time, sure, but Belichick is also one of the best defensive minds of all time. The killer duo of Belichick and Brady ruined many teams' dreams of a title from 2002 to 2019. Since the duo broke up two years back, the Patriots have missed the playoffs and are currently playing ho-hum football in 2021.

5. Washington Football Team: 3 NFL Titles and 3 Super Bowls

Doesn't get much more balanced than that! The Washington Football Team has 3 NFL titles in their record books and 3 Super Bowl wins, as well.

Their first Super Bowl win came in 1982 during a shortened NFL season. The team finished 8-1 and was able to overcome the Lions, Vikings, Cowboys, and Dolphins on their way to their first-ever Super Bowl. Led by star quarterback Joe Theismann and receiver Charlie Brown on offense, the team mostly rode its incredible defense to the title. This defense was led by safety Tony Peters.

Their next title came in 1987, this time over the Denver Broncos by a lopsided score of 42-10. This team was led by dominant receiver Gary Clark on offense and cornerback Barry Wilburn on defense.

Finally, Washington was able to grab the third title in 1991, overcoming the Buffalo Bills by a score of 37-24. This team was dominant. Quarterback Mark Rypien had an awesome season offensively alongside running back Ernest Byner and receiver Gary Clark. Defensively, it was cornerback Darrell Green leading the way for Washington.

Washington has been unable to have any success in the 21st century, making the playoffs just twice in the past six seasons.

4. Pittsburgh Steelers: 6 Super Bowl Wins

The Steelers have been a great team in the NFL for many years. One of the most balanced in terms of Super Bowl victories, the Steelers were able to grab four titles from 1975 to 1980, a dominant stretch that introduced the NFL world to the "Steel Curtain," the name of their dominant defensive line during this stretch. After going silent for most of the 80s and 90s, the Steelers returned in a big way in the 21st century, winning titles in 2005 and 2008.

The 2005 iteration of the Steelers went 11-5, overcoming a stacked Indianapolis team and Seattle Seahawks team to win their first Super Bowl of the 21st century. Led by legendary coach Bill Cowher, young quarterback Ben Roethlisberger, and running back Willie Parker, the Steelers were able to knock off Seattle in a close game. Defensively, the team was led by one of the best safeties of all time: Troy Polamalu.

The 2008 Pittsburgh Steelers and the 2008 Arizona Cardinals met in one of the most closely contested Super Bowl games of all time. The final score was 27-23, with the Steelers just sneaking by the pesky

Cardinals. Ben Roethlisberger once again led the way for Pittsburgh, with Santonio Holmes providing the dramatic, game-winning touchdown catch. Defensively, it was Polamalu and linebacker James Harrison creating trouble.

The Steelers haven't been to a Super Bowl in a while, but this is still one of the most consistent teams in the NFL. It is shocking when Pittsburgh doesn't make the playoffs!

3. Chicago Bears: 7 NFL Titles, 1 Super Bowl

The Chicago Bears, one of the oldest teams in the NFL, were dominant back in the pre-merger, winning an absurd 7 NFL titles before 1967. In Chicago, it has always been about defense. The defense is tough, mean, and will likely try to knock you out of the game if you get too close!

The lone Super Bowl win came in 1985 by one of the most dominant teams in NFL history. Finishing the regular season with a 15-1 record, the Bears ran through the Giants and Rams in the playoffs before matching up with the Patriots in the Super Bowl. Guess what? They ran through the Patriots, too, beating up on the poor New England team by a score of 46-10. The 1985 Bears may have had the best defense in history under coach Mike Ditka. Offensively, Jim

McMahon was reliable and Hall of Famer Walter Payton was excellent, but it was the defense led by defensive end Richard Dent, defensive tackle Steve McMichael, and William "The Refrigerator" Perry that struck fear into opponents. This team was mean.

The Bears have had awesome defenses since then—it's been a staple for them—but they have been trying to find a great quarterback for what feels like decades.

2. New York Giants: 4 NFL Titles, 4 Super Bowl Wins

(Courtesy of unsplash.com.)

The New York Giants were originally named (in part) due to the massive skyscrapers in New York City.

There's always been something special about the New York Giants. Despite having the second most championships of any team, they seem to always be the underdogs. They won 4 NFL Titles in 1927, 1934,

1938, and 1956. From there, they struggled for a long while to gain confidence and find their footing.

The footing was finally found in 1986 when the 14-2 Giants ran over the Denver Broncos to win their first-ever Super Bowl by a score of 39-20. This team was led by legendary coach Bill Parcells, quarterback Phil Simms, and star running back Joe Morris. The team also had a fantastic defense led by defensive end Lawrence Taylor, one of the best linebackers in football history.

The next title came three years later, in 1990. Once again led by Parcells, the Giants were able to get past the feisty Buffalo Bills by a score of 20-19 in the championship game. Phil Simms won his second championship with the team once again leaning on Taylor and linebacker Pepper Johnson.

It would take a while, but the Giants returned to the Super Bowl in 2007, this time facing the tough task of taking down the then-undefeated New England Patriots, a team that many considered to be the best of all time. The 10-6 Giants didn't fret, instead pulling off a miraculous upset of the Patriots by a score of 17-14. This team was led by quarterback Eli Manning, receiver Plaxico Burress, and a rock-solid defense. The game includes one of the most famous catches of all time by David Tyree.

The team would return to the Super Bowl in 2011, once again sporting a basic record of 9-7 and having to beat powerhouses like the Green Bay Packers and San Francisco 49ers just to give them a chance. They got the chance, and it was once again Eli Manning leading the way against Tom Brady and the stacked New England Patriots. Star receivers Victor Cruz and Hakeem Nicks were the main weapons on offense, with defensive end Jason Pierre-Paul causing havoc on defense. It was another close game, but the Giants again beat the Patriots, this time by a score of 21-17. It's hard enough to beat Tom Brady and the Patriots once in a Super Bowl...the Giants were able to do it twice!

Unfortunately, their luck has fallen off since then, as the Giants haven't gone to the playoffs since 2016 when they lost a game to the Packers.

1. Green Bay Packers: 9 NFL Titles and 4 Super Bowl Wins

The most dominant franchise in NFL history is the little team from Green Bay, and it's not even close. Having some of the most legendary coaches of all time helps, for sure, but Green Bay's sustained dominance over such a long history is truly special.

Racking up an incredible 9 NFL titles, the Packers were by far the most dominant team in the pre-AFL-NFL merger.

Once the two merged, the Packers have barely fallen off. Their first title came in the first-ever Super Bowl in 1966. Led by legendary coach Vince Lombardi—who the Super Bowl trophy has since been named after—the 1966 Packers overcame the Chiefs by a dominant score of 35-10 to win the first-ever trophy. Lombardi's team went 12-2 in the regular season before defeating the Cowboys and Chiefs in the playoffs. This team was led by legendary quarterback Bart Starr and a defense that ranked among the best in the league in most categories.

The Packers would come back the following year and win again, this time defeating the Oakland Raiders by a score of 33-14 in the 1967 Super Bowl. Lombardi got yet another championship and the defense was as dominant as ever.

It would be a long while before the Packers would return to the "promised land." It took over three decades, to be exact, but they would eventually find their way back in 1996. Playing against the New

England Patriots for the title, the Packers overcame the Pats by a score of 35-21. A team that was stacked on both offense and defense, this iteration of the Packers was led by star quarterback Brett Favre. Defensively, safety LeRoy Butler was the star with defensive end Reggie White making it hard on quarterbacks, as well.

It would take another decade before Green Bay would win another Super Bowl, this time under star quarterback Aaron Rodgers in 2010. The path to the Super Bowl wasn't easy, with the Packers having to take out the Eagles, Falcons, and Bears to get a chance to square off with a stacked Steelers team. The game was close, but the Packers upended the Steelers by a score of 31-25. Rodgers was the star, but receiver Greg Jennings had an awesome season, too. Defensively, it was cornerback Charles Woodson and linebacker Clay Matthews making things hard on opposing offenses.

The Green Bay Packers may be the most consistent team in NFL history. Despite not making the Super Bowl game since 2010, the Packers are simply expected to show up in the playoffs every season. In fact, since the turn of the 21st century, there have been only a handful of seasons in which the Packers have not made the playoffs. Led by a passionate fanbase, an awesome quarterback in Aaron Rodgers, and a special home-field

advantage at legendary Lambeau Field, the entirety of
the Packers organization is just that: Legendary.

CHAPTER 4

TOP PLAYERS OF ALL TIME

N ow that we have discussed the top franchises of all time, it is time to look at the top individual players of all time. Now, choosing top players in a sport like football is much more challenging than a sport like basketball or hockey. Why? Because the NFL is divided into three highly different aspects of play. There's the offense, there's the defense, and there are the special teams. No element of the game is "more important" than the rest, so choosing a top player across all three facets of the game is quite challenging. Compare this to the NBA, for instance, where every player on the court is forced to play offense and defense simultaneously. The NFL has set positions for offense and defense!

That being said, it is quite possible to go position-by-position and take a look at some of the best to ever do it. That's what we are going to do in this chapter.

From the flashiest quarterbacks to the grittiest offensive linemen, this chapter is going to do a deep dive into each position and pick out some of the best to ever put on a chinstrap! I hope you're as excited as I am.

The Top Players of All Time at Each Position

Quarterback: It seems only right to start with the position that gets the most flair. In no particular order, here are the greatest quarterbacks to ever play the game.

Troy Aikman (1989–2000) Played for the Dallas Cowboys: Compared to some of the other players on this list, Troy Aikman may seem like a bit of an odd addition. Why? Well, there was nothing he did that was particularly flashy, especially when compared to his teammates Emmitt Smith and Michael Irvin. Aikman was often overshadowed by those two teammates. Smith and Irvin are both Hall of Famers who were the very best at what a running back and receiver duo could offer. Thus, the quarterback of the Cowboys in this era, Aikman, probably didn't get the recognition he deserved. This is a little cheap because what Aikman did on the field as a leader and player put him among the best to ever do it at the quarterback position. He was poised, calm, cool, and confident—all traits you want in your quarterback. While his stats are nowhere near as impressive as a Tom Brady or Peyton Manning, Aikman was still able to guide his Cowboys to three Super Bowl victories in just 11 seasons. He was accurate with the ball, made smart decisions, and almost always got his team in a position to potentially win football games. Like all great players, he seemed to play his most confident football when it mattered most. He was 3-0 in the Super Bowl and threw a total of five touchdowns and just one interception in those three games.

Joe Montana (1979–1994) Played for the San Francisco 49ers and Kansas City Chiefs: Joe Montana was so special because he always seemed to play his best football when it mattered the most. Owning four Super Bowl trophies and three Super Bowl Most Valuable Player (MVP) awards, Montana shone the brightest when the lights were on him. He also has the fabulous distinction of never losing a Super Bowl game (4-0). The prototype for all players hoping to make it in the NFL, cool Joe was a special talent. Another important fact about Joe: He was the player who Tom Brady idolized growing up. If Montana wasn't as special a player, maybe the NFL world would've never been given the gift of Tom Brady...something to think about!

Otto Graham (1946–1955) Played for the Cleveland Browns: One of the forgotten legends to play the game, Otto Graham was a three-time NFL champion for the Browns back in the mid-1940s to mid-1950s. A quarterback who truly revolutionized the game with his mix of running and passing, Graham is one of the greatest Cleveland Browns in NFL history. He was inducted into the Hall of Fame in 1965 and was a five-time pro bowler. Quick note, the Pro Bowl is something that happens every year and invites the best players from the regular season from all teams to compete in an All-Star Game. It is considered a high honor, though not as high as a spot in the Hall of Fame!

Peyton Manning (1998–2015) Played for the Indianapolis Colts and Denver Broncos: One of Tom Brady's greatest rivals, Peyton Manning was a phenomenal quarterback who put up some of the greatest statistical seasons of all time. On top of that, he also won two Super Bowls, five MVPs, and has multiple records for passing yards, touchdowns, and other accolades. His greatest accolade likely came in 2013 with the Denver Broncos. That season, he threw for 55 touchdowns and close to 5,500 yards! Those numbers are simply incredible and average out to over three touchdowns a game!

Johnny Unitas (1955–1973) Played for the Pittsburgh Steelers, Baltimore Colts, and San Diego Chargers: Another Colts quarterback making an appearance, here. A Hall of Fame quarterback and four-time NFL champion, Johnny Unitas helped open the door for the Peyton Manning's and Troy Aikman's of the NFL. With the nickname "the Golden Arm," it is not surprising that Unitas held onto the record for most games with a touchdown pass until it was broken by Drew Brees in 2012. That record stood for over 50 years! Fundamental, tough, and incredibly talented, Unitas is considered by many to be the first great quarterback.

(Courtesy of unsplash.com.)

Though he no longer plays for the New England Patriots, Tom Brady will forever be known as a Boston legend. He is one of the most beloved athletes in the history of the sports-rich city, even though he now plays for the Tampa Bay Buccaneers.

Tom Brady (2000–Present) Played for the New England Patriots and Tampa Bay Buccaneers: I know I said this list was going to be in no particular order, but there is a reason why Tom Brady is going last for the quarterbacks. He is practically the undisputed Greatest of All Time at the position, winning more Super Bowls (7) than any other franchise has (NFL titles excluded). Those are simply astounding numbers. The craziest part? He is still doing it today. Despite being in the league for over two decades, Brady is currently leading the entire NFL in passing yards at the time of this book. While he has undoubtedly been surrounded by great coaches, players, and defenses in his career, that doesn't change the fact that Brady is the best quarterback in history. He's a three-time MVP and 13-time Pro-Bowler. The guy is simply unstoppable and is going to be inducted into the Hall of Fame shortly after he retires.

Running Backs:

Barry Sanders (1989–1998) Played for the Detroit Lions: Another running back who had a relatively short career, Barry Sanders was one of the most electrifying players to ever step onto a football field. Considered by many to be the best player to never appear in a Super Bowl, Sanders still earned one league MVP, four trips to the Pro Bowl, and a Hall of Fame induction in 2004. While not a particularly tall or strong man, Sanders used incredible speed, footwork, and skills to move around, through, and even over defenders! In all 10 seasons that he played, he was always a 1,000-yard rusher. Simply put, he was a once-in-a-generation talent.

Emmitt Smith (1990–2004) Played for the Dallas Cowboys: Even with other Hall of Famers Troy Aikman and Michael Irvin stealing touches away from him, Emmitt Smith was still a dominant presence in the Dallas Cowboys offense for over a decade. Owning an MVP award, one Super Bowl MVP, and a spot in the Hall of Fame, Emmitt Smith was nearly unstoppable behind a great Cowboys offensive line. His best season came in 1995 when he rushed for over 1,700 yards, added over 350 more receiving yards, and accounted for 25 total touchdowns! All of those stats are incredible, and so was Emmitt...he is one of the best running backs to ever play the game.

Walter Payton (1975–1987) Played for the Chicago Bears: While Gale Sayers may have set the stage for great Chicago running backs, Walter Payton took the idea and ran with it—literally! He is one of the most consistent running backs of all time, earning a place in the Hall of Fame, while also sporting an MVP and Super Bowl MVP trophy, too. His best season likely came in 1977 when he ran for over 1,800 yards and scored 20 touchdowns. Slick, strong, tough, and fast, it took a whole army to bring this guy down once he got into the open field. As good a man off the field as he was a player on the field, the league eventually created the Walter Payton Man of the Year Award. Considered to be one of the most prestigious honors in the NFL, it is awarded to a player who shows exemplary service off the field.

Jim Brown (1957–1965) Played for the Cleveland Browns: Much like Tom Brady and the list of quarterbacks, though I claimed that the list was in no particular order, it is pretty clear that Jim Brown is the best running back to ever play the game. He's a Hall of Famer, won a Super Bowl, was a three-time MVP, and was simply one of the toughest players to ever put on an NFL jersey. His best season came in 1963 when he accounted for over 2,000 all-purpose yards and 15 touchdowns. Stronger than arguably any other player to ever play the position and with speed to boot, Jim Brown is one of the few players in NFL history that you can confidently say would be able to dominate regardless of the era in which he played.

Wide Receiver:

Randy Moss (1998–2012): Played for the Minnesota Vikings, Oakland Raiders, New England Patriots, Tennessee Titans, and San Francisco 49ers: Though Jerry Rice is likely the greatest wide receiver to ever play the game, Randy Moss wasn't far behind. I will never forget the first season where he and Tom Brady teamed up back in 2007. Though he had better statistical seasons earlier in his career with the Minnesota Vikings, his career resurgence with the New England Patriots was simply incredible to witness. He caught 23 (!) touchdowns to go along with close to 1,500 receiving yards for the Patriots that season. He and Brady were unstoppable. Winning a Super Bowl and being inducted into the Hall of Fame a few years later, Randy Moss will forever be one of the most gifted receivers to ever play the position.

Jerry Rice (1985–2004): Played for the San Francisco 49ers, Oakland Raiders, and Seattle Seahawks: Considered by many to be the second-best offensive player of all time, Jerry Rice won an incredible three Super Bowls alongside his quarterback, Joe Montana, for the San Francisco 49ers. He had some of his best seasons of all time with the 49ers, with his best, in particular, coming in 1995. That year, he recorded over 1,800 receiving yards to go with 15 touchdowns. Big, consistent, tough, and clutch beyond all belief, Jerry Rice was near unguardable whether he was playing with Montana or any other quarterback. He was simply a special talent.

Tight End:

Tony Gonalez (1997–2013): Played for the Kansas City Chiefs and Atlanta Falcons: The greatest tight end of all time is undoubtedly Tony Gonzalez. A great blocker, pass-catcher, and runner of the football, Gonzales was nearly unstoppable and was massively influential in ushering in a new type of tight end to the game. Before Gonzalez, tight ends were historically blocking players and little more. They would occasionally catch a pass, yes, but their number one priority was opening lanes for the running back to run through. Gonzalez changed that. His best season was likely in 2000 as a member of the Kansas City

Chiefs. That season, he caught over 1,200 yards and scored 9 touchdowns. Before him, those numbers would only be seen in wide receivers! A great man on and off the field, Gonzalez was inducted into the Hall of Fame in 2019. Despite never winning a Super Bowl, Gonzalez remains one of the best to ever do it at the tight end position.

Offensive Line:

Forrest Gregg (1956–1971) Played for the Green Bay Packers and Dallas Cowboys: Though offensive linemen never get the same glory as the rest of the offensive players around them, doing anything on offense without these behemoths protecting your quarterback would be impossible. Forrest Gregg, a Hall of Famer and staple of Vince Lombardi's Super Bowl-winning teams, was excellent as both a pass protector and run blocker. He won a total of eight championships stretching from the pre-merger until the early 70s. For those counting at home...yes! That is one more than Tom Brady has won.

<u>Defense</u>

Linebacker:

Lawrence Taylor (1981-1993) Played for the New York Giants: Not only is Lawrence Taylor the greatest linebacker of all time, but he is also likely the greatest defensive player of all time. Epitomizing the phrase "defense wins championships," Taylor was one of the toughest guys to cover in the history of the game. Fast, powerful, and tough, Taylor made it difficult for any offensive lineman to have a chance working against him. He won two championships with the Giants, with his best season likely coming in 1986 when he was able to record 20.5 sacks! While the half-sack stat may look odd for some of you, it is important to note that players can share sacks if they both get to the quarterback. Labeled as likely the hardest-hitting player in history, Lawrence Taylor was one player you didn't want to cross.

Defensive End:

(Courtesy of unsplash.com.)

Reggie White (1985–2000) Played for the Philadelphia Eagles, Green Bay Packers, and Carolina Panthers: Another player who was awesome at getting after the quarterback, many consider Reggie White to be the greatest pass-rusher of all time. At such a violent position, it takes a special kind of toughness to power through the daily grind and continue to get after the quarterback. That was Reggie White. Relentless, fast, and powerful, Reggie White was able to get past almost any lineman and alter the quarterback's plan. His best season came in 1987 when he was able to record 21.0 sacks for the Philadelphia Eagles. A Super Bowl champion, defensive player of the year, and Hall of Famer, Reggie White was able to do it all in his 14-year career.

Defensive Tackle:

Joe Greene (1969–1981) Played for the Pittsburgh Steelers: Anybody with the nickname "Mean" Joe Greene has to be considered one of the best defensive players of all time, right? In Joe Greene's case...yes! A four-time Super Bowl champion with the Pittsburgh Steelers, Joe Green helped set the tone for that amazing line of defenses in Pittsburgh. In other words, he was the main reason behind the Steelers nickname for those seasons: The Steel Curtain. His best season likely came in 1972 when he was able to record

11 sacks to go along with being one of the toughest run stoppers in the league. A no-doubt Hall of Famer and brutal competitor, Joe Greene helped pave the way for the modern-day defensive tackle.

Safety:

Ronnie Lott (1981–1994) Played for the San Francisco 49ers, Los Angeles Raiders, and New York Jets: Another four-time Super Bowl champion, Ronnie Lott was able to make his mark on the league by being a tough hitter, good perimeter defender, and excellent leader. While Joe Montana was the focal point of the team on offense, Lott was holding down the fort on defense. A Hall of Famer, many consider Lott to be the greatest safety of all time. I have a hard time disagreeing!

Cornerback:

Deion Sanders (1989–2000, 2004–2005) Played for the Atlanta Falcons, San Francisco 49ers, Dallas Cowboys, Washington Redskins, and Baltimore Ravens: Before Deion Sanders showed up, the cornerback position was not very glamorous. A lot of people made fun of the position and said it was for those people that couldn't make it as a receiver! Well, Deion "Primetime" Sanders helped change that notion. Fast, powerful, and elusive, Deion Sanders was able to shut down receivers while also being one of the greatest kick returners in NFL history. Once the ball was in his hands, he was nearly impossible to bring down with his combination of elusiveness and speed. In the modern-day NFL, cornerbacks are no longer disrespected like they were before Sanders took the field. He is a two-time Super Bowl champion and a Hall of Famer.

CHAPTER 5

TOP NFL COACHES
OF ALL TIME

While it may seem like the role of the coach is not entirely important after we have spent so much time talking about players, this couldn't be further from the truth. The coach has a ton of duties that go into every NFL game. They have to talk to their team, come up with strategies to prepare for the opponent, come up with unique play calls to move their team down the field, balance the egos of the players, and so much more. Without the coach, the whole operation would fall apart.

So what makes a good coach? Well, the truth of the matter is that there is no perfect blueprint. A coach like Jimmy Johnson, for example, was well-known for having a great relationship with his players and being friends with them. Bill Belichick, on the other hand, is as stoic as they come and focuses much more on things like strategy and culture.

In this chapter, we will look at the 10 greatest coaches of all-time in the NFL. For this list, we will be counting down in order unlike the greatest players at each position!

The Top 10 Greatest Coaches in NFL History

10. Bill Parcells

Clocking in at #10, we have Bill Parcells, nicknamed "Big Tuna." Coaching for 19 years for four different clubs, Parcells was able to win two Super Bowls in his time with the New York Giants. Sporting a 172-130 overall record (11-8 in the playoffs), Parcells is possibly most notable for being the mentor of Bill Belichick (we will hear more about him soon). More than that, however, Parcells was a calm, smart, and powerful force on the sidelines who was able to convey a lot by saying very little. His teams were historically tough on defense. This was of course helped out by the fact that he had Lawrence Taylor on his Giants teams the two years he won Super Bowls with that club.

9. Chuck Noll

The Steelers weren't always the dominant franchise that we came to love over the years. Before Chuck Noll arrived, in fact, they hadn't won a Super Bowl in over 35 years. Then Chuck Noll arrived and they won four in six seasons. A Hall of Famer with an impressive playoff record of 16-8, Chuck Noll epitomized what it meant to be a part of the Steelers' organization. He was tough, loud, mean, and vocal, but he loved his players dearly. The Steelers have since had other awesome coaches like Bill Cowher and Mike Tomlin, but none have been able to replicate the success that Chuck Noll brought to the organization.

8. Tom Landry

Few coaches were more consistent than Tom Landry. Landry coached for an impressive 29 seasons and had a streak of 20 straight with winning records. Pair this with his respectable 20-16 record in the playoffs and you have a legendary Dallas Cowboys head coach. Cool, slick, but tough on the sidelines with his players, you could always tell that Landry had great control over his teams and their decision-making. When it comes to a list of the greatest coaches of all time, none is complete with Landry making an appearance.

7. George Halas

One of the winningest coaches in NFL history, George Halas coached the Bears—the "Monsters of the Midway"—for 40 seasons. Had he coached in the modern-day NFL, his spot on this list would likely be higher. Still, Halas was able to rack up over 300 wins, six NFL titles, and a spot in the Hall of Fame directly after he retired. In Chicago's history, they have always been known for tough, hard-nosed, and physical football play. Halas epitomized these beliefs better than any other coach in the storied franchise's history.

6. Joe Gibbs

A legend among legends, Joe Gibbs won three Super Bowls with three different quarterbacks in his time with Washington. A legacy forged by fantastic defense, Gibbs was consistent, solid, and reliable on the sidelines for the Redskins. A friendly and personable guy, Joe Gibbs was able to coach his teams up with a mix of friendliness and tough love when the need for it arrived. With a 154-94 overall record and 17-7 playoff record, Gibbs was one coach who deserved more respect for what he did for Washington.

(Courtesy of unsplash.com.)

5. Paul Brown

The man behind the name, you know you have made an impact when you have an entire organization named after you (the Cleveland Browns). Winner of seven total championships and a Hall of Famer in 1967, Paul Brown will forever go down as one of the greatest innovators and coaches in NFL history. The most amazing stat that I have to offer about Paul Brown is that he was able to appear in 10 straight title games (!) from a span of 1946 to 1956. His overall record of 213-104 will forever go down as one of the best in football history.

4. Bill Walsh

When you think about the modern-day NFL offense and how it was invented, look no further than

49ers's coach Bill Walsh. Coaching from 1979 to 1988, Walsh was able to start the transition from a run-heavy scheme to a pass-heavy scheme by implementing amazing players such as Joe Montana and Jerry Rice into his offense. Winner of four Super Bowls (4-0), Walsh will always be known to be Montana's second-half. He was fun-loving, cool, and friendly, but wasn't scared to get after you if you were making a mistake. With an overall record of 92-59 and a playoff record of 10-4, Walsh was one of the best playoff coaches in NFL history.

3. Don Shula

Don Shula has the most wins in NFL history as a coach (328). I think there is little more that needs to be said about his legacy! Coaching the 1972 Miami Dolphins, Shula achieved the first and only perfect season in NFL history (17-0). More than that, his overall record of 328-156 speaks for itself. A tough coach on his players, Shula epitomized the old-school style of coaching that was so popular in the 1960s and 1970s. He loved his players, sure, but he also loved winning! With a dominant presence on both offensive and defensive preparation, Shula will forever be known as one of the greatest coaches to ever do it.

2. Vince Lombardi

When you think coach, you should think of Vince Lombardi. With a booming voice, powerful presence, and larger-than-life persona, Lombardi was able to lead his Green Bay Packers to five titles in just eight short seasons. His teams were tough, consistent, and prideful, all traits that go into the Green Bay Packers in general. Unfortunately for Lombardi and the rest of the game, we were never able to see what great things he could've done with the Washington Redskins. Shortly after taking the position in 1969, Lombardi succumbed to colon cancer. A great man, visionary, and fantastic coach, Lombardi is permanently remembered in the league in part due to his name being on the Super Bowl (Lombardi) trophy.

1. Bill Belichick

A polarizing figure for many reasons, Bill Belichick is both the most loved and most hated coach in NFL history depending on who you ask. What can't be said about him by even his most loyal of haters, however, is that he isn't a good football coach. Beginning his career with the Cleveland Browns in 1991, Belichick was able to change his career (and football history) when he joined the New England Patriots in 2000. From there, he was able to team up with Tom Brady to win an incredible six championships in 19 seasons. More than that, Belichick was able to dominate the playoffs in that span, sporting an incredible 31-12 record. While Tom Brady was leading the offense, Belichick was coaching up the defense. Known for his ability to seemingly always take the opposing team's best player completely out of the game, Bill Belichick made beating his Patriots—especially in the playoffs—a nearly impossible task.

CHAPTER 6

RECORDS AND FUN FACTS

W hile I hoped that all of you enjoyed learning a bit about the history of the game and some of the best players to ever play, I think this will be one of the most interesting and engaging chapters in the whole book!

When a league has been around as long as the NFL, you just know that there will be certain records, facts, and interesting tidbits that few people know or realize even exist. That is the purpose of this chapter.

We will be looking at various records, fun facts, and inspiring stories to show you some of the coolest aspects of the NFL that few people even realize are there.

In this chapter, I hope you are able to learn a few interesting things that you can share with your friends, family, and teachers to wow them with your impressive knowledge of the sport!

Records

- In a 1990 game against the Seattle Seahawks, Chiefs player Derrick Thomas was able to **sack quarterback Dave Krieg seven times**. Though some players have gotten relatively close since then, many believe this is one of the most unbreakable records in NFL history.

- Colts' receiver Marvin Harrison **caught an incredible 143 passes** in 2002. With Peyton Manning throwing him the ball, it sometimes looked like the duo was playing a video game!

- A less fun record sees the 1976 Tampa Bay Buccaneers losing **26 straight games** into 1977. Thankfully for Tampa Bay fans, they have since won two Super Bowls in the 21st century.

- Quarterback and kicker George Blanda **played an incredible 26 seasons** of NFL football! While it originally seemed like that record would stay forever, Tom Brady is now in his 21st season and is not looking to be slowing down any time soon.

- Another tough record to have is when you are a quarterback and have the most interceptions ever thrown in a game. That record belongs to Jim Hardy, who **threw eight interceptions in a game** back in 1950.

⊃ Legendary Viking Paul Krause had an incredible **81 career interceptions.** Charles Woodson got close recently with 71.

⊃ Receiver Willie "Flipper" Anderson **caught 15 passes for 336 yards** and a touchdown against the New Orleans Saints. Lions receiver Calvin Johnson got close in 2013, falling just short with 329 yards and a score.

⊃ Legendary quarterback Otto Graham reached **10 straight championship appearances.** Out of all of the NFL records, this one might be the toughest to ever match. Making one Super Bowl is hard...making 10 straight? Nearly impossible.

⊃ The largest TV audience in NFL history was for the 2012 game between the New York Giants and the New England Patriots in the Super Bowl. The audience **reached a peak of 114 million viewers** during Madonna's halftime show.

⊃ The highest completion percentage for a quarterback was **71.2%** by Drew Brees in the 2011 season.

◐ David Akers set a record by **attempting 52 field goals** for San Francisco 49ers in the 2011 season.

◐ A recent NFL record came just a few months back when Baltimore Ravens kicker Justin Tucker launched and connected on a **66-yard field goal** to beat the Detroit Lions. The loss affected the Lions' confidence, as the team is currently the only winless squad in the NFL with a record of 0-8.

(Courtesy of unsplash.com.)

Fun Facts About NFL Players

1. Roger Staubach is the richest NFL player in the world.

A fantastic quarterback with an even bigger pension for great wealth, Roger Staubach is worth an estimated $600 million! The funniest part about this great wealth is that the majority of it didn't even come from his playing days. Though he made a more than fair salary from being the quarterback of the Dallas Cowboys, the main source of his income came from great investments! When he wasn't playing football, he was working as a real estate officer in the off-season. It shows that we all don't have to be incredible athletes to make a ton of money. A few other names in the richest player pool include Peyton Manning, Al Davis, John Madden, and Steve Young.

2. Brett Favre committed the most fumbles of all time.

It's funny, I was initially thinking that the player with the most fumbles of all time would be a running back! After all, these are the players who are running the ball up the field against linebackers, safeties, and cornerbacks all trying to punch the ball out. Instead, the player with the most fumbles in the history of the game is legendary quarterback Brett Favre. Favre had the reputation of being a bit of a "free thrower," meaning he would chuck the ball downfield with free reign. This resulted in defensive ends and linebackers having more time to get to him and force the ball out of his hands. All told, he committed 166 fumbles. Other NFL players with a boatload of fumbles include Eli Manning, Warren Moon, Dave Krieg, and Kerry Collins.

3. **Charles Haley has the second most Super Bowl rings.**

It's no surprise that Tom Brady has the most Super Bowl rings of all time with seven. What's slightly more surprising, however, is that linebacker Charles Haley has the second most! Playing with the San Francisco 49ers and Dallas Cowboys in the 1980s and 1990s, Haley was able to rack up four titles with the 49ers and one with the Cowboys. Not bad for a player that many diehard fans have never even heard of! A few other players with many rings include Joe Montana, Bill Romanowski, Ted Hendricks, Marv Fleming, and Matt Millen.

4. **Antonio Cromartie has the most children of any NFL player with 14.**

I love this fact because it is so appalling and random! While many people in the United States are overwhelmed with the idea of having even three children, Antonio Cromartie has 14 (!) kids to his name. I can't even imagine thinking of trying to keep an eye on all of those kids at one time! Though slightly less egregious, Philip Rivers has nine kids.

5. **Odell Beckham Jr. has the most Instagram followers.**

With over 14 million followers, Odell Beckham Jr. of the Cleveland Browns takes the cake as the most popular NFL player on Instagram. The popular social media site hero is well-known for sharing photos of himself and various videos about the amazing catches he can make on the football field.

6. **Michael Vick was drafted by the Colorado Rockies.**

Though it is not uncommon for NFL players to get some looks from MLB teams based on their strong arm talent and overall athleticism, I was surprised to learn that Michael Vick joined the list here. An incredible athlete who was able to run at great speeds and chuck the ball downfield from his quarterback position, Vick was drafted in the 30th round by the Rockies despite having quit baseball in the eighth grade! He never considered playing, but this is still a great honor nevertheless.

7. **Robert Griffin III has a sock collection.**

Though it is no surprise that NFL players love to have hobbies and collections much like us, you usually think that players would have shoe collections or hat collections. Instead, Robert Griffin III, a former quarterback who is now an announcer, has an amazing sock collection. With styles including Angry Birds, SpongeBob SquarePants, and Cookie Monster, Robert Griffin III is not afraid to show off his quirkier side with his massive collection!

8. **Joe Montana and John Candy "team up" at a Super Bowl.**

Cool Joe lived up to his nickname before embarking on a game-winning drive against the Cincinnati Bengals back in Super Bowl XXIII. Talking with Harris Barton, Joe pointed out that John Candy was on the sidelines. For those of you who are unaware who John Candy was, he was one of the most famous comedians and actors of the 1980s and 1990s with roles in huge movies such as *Planes, Trains, and Automobiles* (1987) and *Spaceballs* (1987). The fact that Montana was able to be so cool at that moment and not worry about the game but instead have the wherewithal to point out a comedian in the stands is a testament to how little Joe Montana felt pressure.

9. Calvin Johnson and Roman Reigns were on the same college roster.

One of the most dominant receivers in the history of the NFL was Calvin Johnson ("Megatron"). Physical, tough, and incredibly strong, Johnson was borderline unguardable in his peak seasons. While he set all kinds of records in his NFL career, there is an interesting, lesser-known fact about him and WWE star Roman Reigns. WWE, otherwise known as professional wrestling, is oftentimes paired alongside the NFL when talking about the most popular sports in America. The two beasts played together at Georgia Tech! The 2006 Yellow Jackets' squad had both the stars on the roster, with Johnson turning into a future Hall-of-Famer and Reigns becoming one of the top wrestlers in the world.

10. Richard Sherman is a salutatorian.

When we think about football players, we don't often think about good grades. The stigma surrounding NFL players is that they slacked off in college and got through classes mostly because of their status as football players. While this is likely true for some players, don't put Richard Sherman in that category! Sherman was the salutatorian in his high school class at Dominguez High School and later went on to attend (and graduate from) Stanford. Though Sherman would later gain fame for a particularly vocal interview with Erin Andrews following a win over the San Francisco 49ers, make no mistake about it: Sherman is a smart cookie.

11. Wes Welker owns a racehorse named Undrafted.

This one goes a little deeper and I will need to fill in the holes for you before this will make sense. Every year, there is a draft in the NFL. This includes great players from college who are looking to join the league. The draft has seven rounds with 32 players being drafted in each round. After some quick math, this comes out to 216 players being picked each year!

After that, the rest of the players who do not hear their name called can be picked up by teams as 'undrafted'" players. There is a negative stigma surrounding undrafted players, as they "weren't good enough" to be picked in the original draft and are often disrespected.

Wide receiver Wes Welker was one of those undrafted players but would go on to win multiple Super Bowls with the Patriots and Denver Broncos. To keep the chip on his shoulder, Welker owns a racehorse named Undrafted to remind himself of the many teams that passed on him in the drafting process.

Fun Facts about the NFL

(Courtesy of unsplash.com)

1. **Besides Thanksgiving, the most food that Americans eat on a single day each year is Super Bowl Sunday:** This one isn't too surprising. I would have guessed that Christmas is likely close to the top of that list, as well! Super Bowl Sunday is practically a national holiday at this point, with buffalo wings being the food of choice! Beyond that, it is a time where many parties happen across the country. Everyone knows that the more people there are in a space, the more likely it is people will eat a huge amount of food. Eating is inherently social, so the fact that Super Bowl Sunday has so much food devoured is not at all surprising.

2. **Back in 2011, it cost any given business \$3.0 million for a 30-second-long commercial in the Super Bowl:** There are different kinds of people who exist at any given Super Bowl party. Some are there simply to watch the game. They love football, respect the game, and enjoy seeing the two best teams duke it out to see who comes out on top. Since the Super Bowl halftime show was implemented, there is a group of people that love to watch the spectacle and the music. Others are there to watch the game simply for the commercials! Considering

how much money is spent to put a commercial up for the Super Bowl, it is not surprising that companies usually go all-out with that many eyes on the screen for comedy purposes or entertainment value. The Super Bowl commercials rarely disappoint!

3. **All footballs used in games come from a Wilson plant in Ada, Ohio:** Ohio and football go hand-in-hand. The Hall of Fame is located there, the Browns and Bengals are located there, and the factory that creates all game-day footballs is located there, too! Considering that this plant is used solely for making NFL footballs, it is no surprise that they are incredibly busy during the season.

4. **The Green Bay Packers are the only team to win three straight championships in history:** They did this during the 1960s under legendary coach Vince Lombardi. Many teams have won two straight since then, but no team has been able to replicate the success that Lombardi had halfway through the 20th century.

5. **Gale Sayers was the youngest Hall of Famer in history:** Injuries cut legendary running back Gale Sayers' career short, but that

didn't stop him from being the youngest player (34) to ever be inducted into the Hall of Fame. Many players are still in the midst of their careers at that age, not being enshrined into the Hall of Fame! It is a testament to how good Sayers was at the peak of his career to be able to receive this honor.

6. **Offensive holding used to be a 15-yard offense:** This is a hot-button issue, as many people in the NFL believe that 10 yards is too much for holding and that it should be dropped to 5! Holding is when an offensive lineman holds a defender without letting go. While you are allowed to block, which is putting your hands out and pushing the defender away from you. You are not able to grab onto the defender and impede his movement. Up until 1975, holding was a 15-yard penalty! That is a considerable offense, as that means a run that went for 50 yards would have to come back to the original line of scrimmage plus an additional 15 yards in the other direction. It is not surprising that this rule was eventually changed to help the offense.

7. **Brett Favre's first completed pass was to himself:** There is a rare play in football where

the quarterback will throw a pass and it will ricochet off a defensive or offensive player in front of him. The ball will then bounce back in his direction. At this moment, the player is allowed to catch his pass! It is rarely seen in the game, so it is even rarer that legendary quarterback Brett Favre's first completed pass was to Brett Favre!

8. **The Arizona Cardinals own the largest playoff drought in history:** There was a time from 1947 to 1998 when the Cardinals made exactly zero playoff appearances. The drought—51 years to be exact—is the longest in history.

9. **It took the New Orleans Saints 35 years to win their first playoff game:** Another team that is a modern-day powerhouse, the Saints struggled for years to win even a single playoff game.

10. **Since 1988, every team, except Houston, has played in a conference championship game:** This is an incredible stat as it shows how quickly the league turns over. The only team that has never played in a conference championship game is the Houston Texans, the newest team in the NFL.

11. **Ed Sabol was the oldest Hall of Fame inductee:** He was 98 years old or 64 years older than the youngest Hall of Fame inductee, Gale Sayers!

12. **Sammy Baugh once led the league in passing, punting, and defensive interceptions in the same season:** This came back when players would play multiple positions. Though this phenomenon has since nearly disappeared, Shohei Otani of the Los Angeles Angels over in the MLB is a player who both hits and pitches. Who knows...maybe this trend will make it back to the NFL?

13. **The Chicago Bears have the most retired jersey numbers with 13:** When a player has a phenomenal career, one of the largest honors he can get from a team is having his jersey retired. This means the jersey will hang in the rafters and no other player will be able to use that number. The Bears have 13 of these jerseys retired, more than any other team.

14. **In 1992, the league experimented with two bye weeks:** A bye week is when a team can take a week off from playing a game. This was implemented due to the high number of injuries that were occurring in the early stages

of the league. While injuries still happen, the bye week helps in alleviating some of the pressure on the tired muscles of the players. In 1992, the league tested out the idea of two bye weeks. It didn't stay around for long.

15. **Steve Young is the only lefty quarterback in the Hall of Fame:** This one is downright shocking! Although lefties are rare by nature, it would appear that more than one lefty quarterback would be in the Hall of Fame, right? Wrong. Steve Young is the only player to have this honor.

16. **Football passed baseball as "America's Pastime" in 1965:** Though baseball continues to use the name!

17. **The Indianapolis Colts won 23-straight regular-season games from 2008 to 2009:** Led by Hall of Fame quarterback Peyton Manning, the Colts were quite literally unstoppable in this remarkable stretch.

18. **The Steelers have the most wins since the AFL/NFL Merger:** This one was a little surprising, as I would assume it would be the Green Bay Packers. Alas, most of the Packers' damage came before the two leagues merged in 1967.

19. **Tom Brady threw just four interceptions back in 2010 for the New England Patriots:** Because, of course, he is Tom Brady. Though many are saying that Brady could be in the midst of his best season in 2021, he has already thrown five interceptions on the year and we are not even halfway through the season.

20. **The 1992 Chargers are the only team to make the playoffs after starting 0-4:** You are supposed to never say never in football, but starting 0-4 is close to a death sentence.

21. **The Minnesota Vikings have the best home record since the AFL/NFL Merger:** Oddly enough, the Vikings are one of the few franchises that have never won a Super Bowl. Maybe if all of the games were played in Minnesota, they would have as many titles as the Packers!

Inspiring Stories About the NFL

There's a common misconception regarding the NFL that it is simply a league of brutes who go around trying to injure other players. There is no heart involved, no brains involved, and no love involved. In reality, this couldn't be further from the truth. Making it to the NFL is hard. Players, from a young age, need to have the drive, perseverance, finances, family support, and love from their community to even have a chance to make it on an NFL roster. The NFL is the best of the best, and it shouldn't be taken lightly. We can sometimes take the tremendous talent of these players for granted and forget that we are watching some of the greatest athletes in the world compete for the Lombardi Trophy.

While some players have an easier path to the league, others have to battle tooth and nail just to get the smallest sliver of a chance to break in. If your father was an NFL player, for instance, you will have a much easier path to the league than a poor kid from Compton, California.

In this section, we will take a brief look at a few inspiring stories about the NFL. While I feel like we have covered a ton of awesome information to this point, I feel like the majority of it has been having to do with stats and fun information. In this section, we will go for a little heart!

(Courtesy of unsplash.com.)

Michael Oher

The story of Michael Oher is well-documented. It is so well-documented that the hit movie *The Blind Side* was based on the story of Oher. The film starred Sandra Bullock and came out in 2009.

Oher came from a tough upbringing as one of 11 children to Denise Oher and Michael Williams. His mother battled crack addiction while he was just a child, and his father was in and out of prison for many years of his life. Eventually, his father was killed in prison, which resulted in Michael Oher being moved from one foster family to another.

He eventually settled in with a foster family that recommended he sign up for Briarcrest Christian

School. Finding a passion for high school football, Oher began to attract the attention of NFL scouts who believed he had the potential to make it into the NFL. Scouts are people from NFL teams who go out and look for talent to add to their team.

There was one issue, however: Oher had terrible grades. Never learning the importance of school and grades growing up, Oher was focusing much more on football than he was in the classroom. With the help of his teachers and foster family, he began to work towards raising his GPA and enrolling in an NCAA program. Eventually, through hard work and perseverance, he was able to get his grades to a solid standing.

From there, he enrolled in the University of Mississippi, where he began to attract the attention of even more NFL scouts. With a huge frame of 6-4 and 315 pounds, Oher quickly became one of the top offensive linemen in the collegiate circuit. He was eventually drafted in the first round of the 2009 NFL Draft by the Baltimore Ravens and played in the league for close to a decade.

Perhaps even more impressive? Oher was able to secure a criminal justice degree from the University of Mississippi. Going from a young orphan to an NFL player and college graduate is a story that doesn't happen often, but Oher's toughness and perseverance made it possible.

Tom Brady

While Tom Brady is now considered to be one of the greatest football players in the history of the sport, it wasn't always that way when he first began his football experience. Having a pure love for the game and an intense idolization for Joe Montana, Brady separated himself early on from the rest of the pack based on his love for the sport rather than love for potential fame and money.

In high school, Brady was more well-known as a baseball player than a football player! Playing catcher, he was eventually drafted in the 18th round of the MLB draft by the Montreal Expos.

And that wasn't all. A professional team in Canada also showed interest in Brady and his powerful arm early on in his high school career, offering him a lucrative contract to come play on the other side of the border. Determined to follow the path of Montana and the other greats, however, Brady declined and instead focused on betting on himself.

Eventually, he ended up at the University of Michigan, the Wolverines, where he was barely given any playing time across his multi-year career. Dealing with depression and anxiety at this time and disappointed in his spot with the University of Michigan, Brady reached out to numerous professionals to help deal with his anxiety.

Instead of burying his head and giving up, however, Brady began to work with the higher-ups at the University of Michigan and eventually won the starting job in his last couple of seasons. He worked so hard that he was given the moniker of team captain, a high honor that only goes to the players who show exceptional leadership both on and off the field.

Even with some impressive numbers at Michigan, it still took until the sixth round for an NFL team to pull the trigger and draft Brady. That team? The New England Patriots. What has followed has been one of the greatest careers in NFL history.

If things had gone slightly differently and Brady had given up when things had looked bleak early on at Michigan and potentially tried a different career, this would've altered the history of football as we know it.

Jay Bromley

With a similar start to his life to Michael Oher, Jay Bromley was born to a mother who had crack issues and a father who was in and out of prison for the first couple years of Jay's life.

Growing up, Bromley played football at Flushing High School where he showed a ton of talent in a limited time. As a senior, he recorded 12 sacks and 60 tackles—some incredible numbers for a high schooler! Unfortunately for Bromley, he was not offered a spot on a single collegiate football team following his incredible season. Instead of being demotivated and wanting to quit, Bromley put his head down and continued to work on improving his game.

Scouts thought Bromley was too slow, had poor technique, and apparently his build was not athletic enough to earn him a spot on any team.

Again, instead of quitting, he took a spot at the Outback Steakhouse Empire Challenge, a circuit that showed some of the best high school players in the nation. Winning the MVP trophy for the game, an official offer finally appeared. He was approached by Syracuse University and Jay took his chance with the Orange.

Once he was at Syracuse, Bromley took off. He got faster, stronger, worked on his technique, and became one of the top defensive players in the country. Following his great career with Syracuse, the New York

Giants offered him a spot on their team in the third round of the 2014 NFL Draft. Bromley would wind up playing in the NFL for five seasons.

Doug Baldwin Jr

Doug Baldwin Jr. joined his first football team when he was just six years old. And then he quit because he was scared to get hit! Baldwin's mother warned him that if he signed up the next season, she wouldn't allow him to quit. Sure enough, he joined the next season and wanted to quit. His mother didn't allow him to do so, saying that quitting was no longer an option.

A highly religious individual, Baldwin carried the importance of his faith with him as he approached high school and eventually college.

Playing for Stanford University, Baldwin would be tested in his faith and penchant for overcoming adversity in his junior year at college. An ankle sprain put him on the bench, and he was caught up with choosing a major and disappointed that his coach had benched him early on in practice. Calling his parents every night to tell them that he wanted to quit Stanford and quit football, his mother instilled the confidence necessary by reverting to her faith and her belief in him. She didn't allow him to quit, and her full confidence in her son to overcome whatever obstacles he was dealing with.

Working harder than ever to improve on his game and get drafted, there was more disappointment awaiting when he went undrafted following a successful senior season at Stanford. He was picked up three days later by the Seattle Seahawks as an undrafted free agent.

Determined to show his worth in his first season with the Seahawks, Baldwin had to battle through injuries and was never able to get going in his first season with Seattle. Sticking with it, however, Baldwin was able to turn it around in his second season with Seattle and only got better from there. He went on to enjoy an incredible eight-year career with the team, winning a Super Bowl and building a great rapport with quarterback Russell Wilson.

Once Baldwin's career was over, he launched numerous charities and organizations to help young people learn the rules of football and better the communities around him. Seen as an approachable, kind, and welcoming soul, Baldwin is a relatable, fun, and awesome person who was also incredibly talented on the football field.

Devin McCourty

Playing alongside his brother Jason at high school, the two brothers eventually took their talents to the University of Rutgers to play together for the Scarlet Knights. While his brother took to the field right away, Devin had to sit on the bench for his first season with Rutgers.

Devin refused to let the disappointment of seeing his teammates take the field without him get the better of him, and he got down to work to improve. He lifted more weights, worked harder on his footwork, and improved his hands.

Raised by a single mother and a brother, Larry, who was much older than the pair (17 years), McCourty's mother instilled the importance of spirituality in the duo from a young age. It became a huge part of their lives and confidence moving forward.

Working hard to improve his game following the disappointment of his forgotten freshman season, Devin improved and eventually played alongside his brother, Jason, at the University of Rutgers. The two both eventually got drafted as well. Jason went to play with the Tennessee Titans, while Devin was drafted by the New England Patriots.

Devin has since become one of the best safeties in the entire league, playing with the Patriots for 11 years (and counting) and winning numerous Super Bowl titles.

He even reconnected with his brother, Jason, for three seasons on the Patriots. His perseverance following a disappointing first season with Rutgers is well-documented and shows the strong will of Devin.

(Courtesy of unsplash.com.)

CHAPTER 7

BEST UNDERDOG
WINS OF ALL TIME

Everybody loves a good underdog story. Whether it is Cinderella, Forrest Gump, the Avengers, or Harry Potter, our society has an infatuation with somebody or something not expected to have a chance who winds up having a chance. There is something dramatic about this phenomenon, and football is no different.

After all, Tom Brady wasn't always the dominant player we know and love today. No, back in 2001, Brady was a no-name quarterback guiding a Patriots team to do battle with the "Greatest Show on Turf" St. Louis Rams. The Rams were heavily favored in the Super Bowl, but Brady won the first-ever Super Bowl for the Patriots. Nowadays, anybody going against Brady is considered a massive underdog!

145

In this chapter, we will be looking at the times in NFL history when underdogs overcame the odds and took down a team that was heavily favored to beat them. This is a special moment whenever it occurs, so try and enjoy the drama of these performances. Nobody thought these teams had a chance and yet they pulled it off! There is something magical about a moment like that.

The Greatest Upset Wins of All Time

Chiefs Overcome Vikings in Super Bowl IV

There is no denying that the AFL was highly disrespected when its teams entered the league following the AFL/NFL merger. NFL teams were considered to be heavily favored in these games with the AFL teams being their "younger brother." This was the case in Super Bowl IV when the AFL Kansas City Chiefs did battle with the NFL Minnesota Vikings.

Posting a 12-2 record during the regular season, the Vikings squared off with the 11-3 Chiefs in a game that was supposed to go Minnesota's way. Instead, the Chiefs had other plans. Following an incredible performance from wide receiver Otis Taylor and a defense that was able to limit the Vikings to just 239 yards of offense, the Chiefs jumped out to a 16-0 lead and never looked back.

Minnesota would answer with a touchdown late in the game, but the damage was already done. The Chiefs won the game 23-7 and proved that the AFL teams were nothing to laugh at.

While not the single biggest upset in history, the Chiefs winning by 16 was shocking against a team that was simply amazing during the regular season.

Vikings Take Down the 49ers in 1987

Few teams were as dominant on paper as the 1987 San Francisco 49ers. Dealing with Joe Montana was hard enough, but dealing with Joe Montana and a new, rising receiver in Jerry Rice? Impossible. Or so many thought.

Instead, the Minnesota Vikings, who were just 9-7 going into the game, were able to start fast against one of the greatest regular season 49ers teams in history. The 49ers coming into the game were favored by 11.0 points by Vegas, meaning the experts believed the San Francisco 49ers were going to win...and relatively easily!

The game started innocently enough, with the Vikings and 49ers exchanging field goals early on in the first quarter. The game then shifted momentum when the Vikings scored 17 straight points including an interception touchdown by Najee Mustafaa against the great Joe Montana. The 49ers would make it close late, but the Vikings eventually pulled away and won the game by a score of 36-24. While the 49ers were favored by 11 to win the game, it wound up being the Vikings taking it by 12!

Quarterback Wade Wilson for the Vikings not only played well, but he outplayed both Joe Montana and Steve Young, two of the best quarterbacks to ever play the game.

The Vikings defense was also able to limit star running back Roger Craig to just 7 carries for 17 yards. It was an incredible performance by a team that very few people gave any chance against the monstrous 49ers.

Super Bowl XXV

The Giants always have a little magic in them when it comes to the playoffs. Facing off against the high-flying Buffalo Bills offense, the Giants had a backup quarterback in Jeff Hostetler doing battle with a team that had some incredible offensive weapons.

Not only this, but late in the second quarter the Giants found themselves trailing the Bills by a score of 16-3. While many teams would roll over and die in this scenario, the Giants battled back and made it 16-10 going into halftime. Then, in the second half, the defense took over. Stymying star quarterback Jim Kelly and making things hard on him, the Giants were able to outscore the Bills 10-3 in the second half to win on a late field goal by Matt Bahr to secure the victory.

Favored by 6.5 coming into the game, the Bills were unable to get past their Super Bowl demons and have not been able to win a Super Bowl since.

Jaguars Announce Their Arrival in 1996

One of the greatest upsets in football history came after the 1996 season when the new kids on the block in the Jacksonville Jaguars marched into Mile High Stadium and took out the number one seeded Denver Broncos led by John Elway and Mike Shanahan, a legendary duo.

There were a few incredible pieces of information to consider when looking at this game. First, the Broncos were favored by 12.5 over the Jaguars, a massive spread! Second, the Broncos got off to a quick start thanks to two touchdowns and a 12-0 lead.

Instead of cracking, however, the Jaguars muscled back and took a 13-12 lead before halftime. From there, it was a back-and-forth battle between heavyweights as the team's traded blows in the entire second half. While Denver would score late, it wouldn't be enough as the Jaguars would hold on to a 30-27 win in one of the hardest stadiums to play!

A tight game all the way through, Jaguars QB Mark Brunell had the game of his life, throwing for two touchdowns and over 240 yards against a tough Broncos defense. Running back Natrone Means rushed for 140 yards and a touchdown, finishing with more yards than Hall of Famer Terrell Davis for the Broncos.

Defensively, the Jaguars were able to do just enough to keep Elway, Davis, and star tight end, Shannon Sharpe, from taking over the game.

Though the Jaguars were riding high following this victory, it wasn't enough to carry them to a Super Bowl, as they bowed down to the New England Patriots the following game by a score of 20-6.

Super Bowl XXXII

Instead of hanging their head following the disappointing loss to the Jacksonville Jaguars a year prior, the Broncos came back in 1997 with a vengeance, going 12-4 in the regular season. They got another shot at Jacksonville that year in the first round of the playoffs, this time dismantling the team by a score of 42-17. They then went on to defeat the Pittsburgh Steelers and Kansas City Chiefs to get a shot at the Green Bay Packers in the 1998 Super Bowl. This Packers team, coming off a Super Bowl win a year prior, had all the tools for a repeat.

Favored by 11 in the game, the Packers began the game quickly with a great score early on to take a 7-0 lead. From there, the Broncos battled and battled, chipping away and eventually taking a 24-17 lead late in the third quarter. The Packers refused to yield, however, and tied the game at 24 from a pass from Brett Favre to Antonio Freeman. From there, the Broncos got the game-winning touchdown rush from legendary running back Terrell Davis to seal the victory.

The game was tight throughout, with quarterback John Elway struggling in the late part of his storied career. He threw for just 123 yards and an interception in the game. Thankfully for Denver, however, they were able to lean on star running back Terrell Davis, as he finished the game with 157 yards rushing and three touchdowns. Defensively, Brett Favre still had a great day for the Packers with three passing touchdowns, but he threw a key interception to help the Broncos hold on.

It was a fantastic game and considered by many to be one of the best Super Bowls of all time.

Super Bowl XXXVI

We alluded to this game earlier, but it bears mentioning in terms of the greatest upsets in NFL history. Led by a then no-named quarterback (Tom Brady) and having battled through incredibly tough opponents like the Oakland Raiders and Pittsburgh Steelers just to have a chance at the Super Bowl, the 2001 New England Patriots were not given much of a chance against the powerful and favored St. Louis Rams. The Rams were led by star quarterback Kurt Warner and went an incredible 14-2 during the regular season. They then ran over the Green Bay Packers and Philadelphia Eagles to do battle with this young and unproven New England Patriots squad.

Favored in the game by two touchdowns (14 points), the Rams found themselves shocked early with a 14-3 deficit going into halftime. Whatever strategy Bill Belichick was deploying against the Rams offense, it was working wonders!

Thankfully for the Rams, they figured it out late in the third quarter and came storming back to tie the game at 17 with just 1:30 left on the game clock. From there, the legend of Tom Brady began with the young quarterback marching his offense down into field goal range before handing the keys over to kicker Adam Vinatieri. Vinatieri connected on the 48-yard field goal try to secure the win against the heavily-favored Rams squad.

Brady was efficient in the game, throwing for 145 yards and a score with zero interceptions. Meanwhile, the Rams star quarterback Kurt Warner threw for close to 350 yards, but also had two untimely interceptions, with one being returned for a touchdown. Belichick was also shockingly able to keep star running back Marshall Faulk contained.

This shocking victory would set off the Patriots train, as they would go on to win five more Super Bowls in the next two decades.

Super Bowl XLII

Football has a funny way of giving and then taking away. While the Patriots were able to pull off the incredible upset in 2001 against a heavily favored Rams squad, they found themselves in the heavily favored position a few years later for Super Bowl XLII against the New York Giants.

Widely considered to be one of the greatest football teams of all time, the 2007 Patriots went a perfect 16-0 in the regular season before running past the Jaguars and Chargers in the playoffs that year. The final hurdle the 18-0 Patriots had to clear was a battle with Eli Manning and the 13-6 Giants...a team that needed to battle tightly with the Bucs, Cowboys, and Packers just to have a shot at the big game.

Entering the game, the Patriots were favored by a staggering 12.5 points. The Giants got the scoring started off of a field goal, but the Patriots quickly answered with a Laurence Maroney touchdown run to make the score 7-3. From there, David Tyree caught a touchdown pass early in the 4th quarter to regain the lead. With the score at 10-7, Brady was able to find star receiver Randy Moss late to gain a 14-10 lead with just 2:30 remaining on the clock. The rest, as they say, was history.

Eli Manning manufactured one of the most legendary drives in football history, showing incredible toughness, guts, and energy to make great play after great play. Eventually, with just 35 seconds remaining, he found Plaxico Burress for a 13-yard touchdown pass. Thus ended the Patriots' bid at the second-ever perfect season.

Tom Brady was as solid as ever, throwing for over 260 yards and a touchdown but losing a costly fumble. Surprisingly, the Giants were able to limit Randy Moss to just five catches for 62 yards...small numbers compared to the rest of his monster season.

For the Giants, Eli Manning threw for over 250 yards and a touchdown but also had an interception.

Star defensive rushers Michael Strahan and Justin Tuck combined for three sacks against Brady.

Watching this game from home with a bunch of New England Patriots fans, it remains one of the most shocking and incredible games ever played.

Super Bowl III

Another famous game, this one involved the AFL New York Jets doing battle with the NFL-favorite, the Baltimore Colts. Led by Broadway Joe Namath, who famously guaranteed a Jets victory, the Jets entered the game with an 11-3 record. The Baltimore Colts were 13-1 in the regular season and were coached by the legendary Don Shula. The Colts dismantled the Cleveland Browns in the game before by a score of 34-0 to have a chance to play the Jets in the Super Bowl.

Shockingly, the Colts were favored in this game by 18 points, one of the highest spreads in NFL playoff history. It didn't start well for the Colts' high-powered offense, however, with the Jets taking a quick 7-0 lead into halftime. From there, the Jets would score 9 more points and have a 16-0 lead going into the 4th quarter. The Colts would score late to make the score a touch more respectable, but this was a dominant performance by Namath and the rest of his New York Jets.

Broadway Joe threw for over 200 yards in the game, an incredible stat for the team, but more shocking was the Jets' ability to intercept Johnny Unitas and the Baltimore Colts four times (!) in the game.

Despite being heavily favored and having one of the best quarterback-coach duos of all time, this game shows you that you should never count your chickens before they hatch. The Jets, against all odds, handed it to the Baltimore Colts.

The Jets Overcome the Rams

A more recent addition to this list, this massive 2020 upset is the biggest upset since 1995 in terms of Vegas odds. Favored in the game by an obscene 17.5 points, the Rams took on the Jets in week 15 of the regular season. Sporting an impressive 9-4 record at the time of the game, the Rams were playing at home against the 0-13 New York Jets. Few expected it to be a close game.

Instead, the Jets came out with firepower early, jumping out to a 13-0 lead thanks to a Ty Johnson touchdown and two Sam Ficken field goals. Rams' kicker Matt Gay was able to slam home a 45-yard field goal at the halftime buzzer to at least get the Rams on the board going into halftime.

The second half was a much different story, with the Rams rallying from being down 20-3 midway through the third quarter to get the score to 23-20 with six minutes plus remaining in the fourth quarter. Unfortunately, that would be the last scoring of the game, as the Rams would eventually fall to the Jets by a final score of 23-20.

Young Jets quarterback Sam Darnold had one of his best games as a pro against the elite Rams defense, throwing for over 200 yards and a touchdown with zero interceptions. On the other side, Rams quarterback Jared Goff struggled, throwing an interception and taking three sacks.

This game would spell the beginning of the end of Goff's time with the Rams, as the team would sputter late in the season before getting eliminated by the Packers in the playoffs. In the offseason, the Rams traded Jared Goff to the Detroit Lions to bring in star quarterback Matthew Stafford.

The 2018 Dolphins Shock the Patriots

This will forever go down as one of the most shocking games in NFL history. While far from a terrible football team, few gave the Miami Dolphins any sort of chance of knocking off the tough New England Patriots at the end of the 2018 season. Vegas had the Patriots favored by 17.5 points despite the two teams having somewhat similar records. What ensued was one of the craziest, most highly competitive, and most shocking games in NFL history.

The game started innocently enough, with the Patriots owning a 27-21 lead over the Dolphins at halftime. From there, it appeared that the Patriots were going to have one of their classic victories in which a last-second field goal doomed the opposing team. Tom Brady marched down the field and got the Patriots into position to win by setting up a 22-yard field goal with just 16 seconds remaining. The Patriots owned a 33-28 lead and appeared to be well on their way to a 10-3 record.

Unfortunately for New England, Miami had other ideas. With just seven seconds remaining in the game, Miami quarterback Ryan Tannehill threw the ball downfield to receiver Kenny Stills. At around the 50-yard line, Stills lateraled the ball back to receiver DeVante Parker. A lateral is a fully legal play where one player throws the ball behind them to another player on the same team. Though it doesn't happen often, it is a legal play! Parker then ran up the field about 10 yards before lateraling the ball back to running back Kenyan Drake. Drake then ran the remainder of the 40 yards and scored a game-winning touchdown! What would later be known as the "Miami Miracle" marked one of the greatest upsets (and endings) in NFL history.

Alas, it wouldn't mean much in the end. The Patriots were able to rebound and win the Super Bowl against the Rams just a few months later.

The Bills Lay the Smackdown on the Vikings

Another game in which the home team was favored by over 17 points, this early season clash between the Buffalo Bills and Minnesota Vikings is one of the most shocking in recent memory. The Vikings, coming off a few playoff appearances and high hopes for their season, invited the rebuilding Buffalo Bills into their home stadium, one of the toughest places to play in the entire league. Few gave the Bills any sort of chance. What followed was a bashing that the Vikings hadn't seen in years.

Buffalo jumped out to a quick lead, leading the Vikings 27-0 at halftime. It was a stunning development and one that had many Viking fans heading for the exits early. The Vikings would be able to score a touchdown late to make the score 27-6, but that is where the final would wind up. It was an amazing performance and one that couldn't be explained by anyone.

Young Buffalo Bills quarterback Josh Allen was fantastic, while veteran quarterback Kirk Cousins struggled mightily against the stingy Buffalo Bills defense. The Vikings would go on to miss the playoffs this season while Buffalo also struggled the rest of the way and finished 6-10.

However, fast forward a few years to today and the Vikings are a middle-of-the-pack team while the Bills are considered to be one of the best in football. Time flies!

Washington Beats America's Team in 1995

There is no denying that the 1995 Dallas Cowboys team was one of the best ever. They won the Super Bowl that year and are highly considered to be one of the toughest teams to stop on offense in the last 30years.

One of the teams to defeat them in that special season? The no-name Washington Redskins! At the time of the game, the Cowboys were 10-3 while the Redskins were just 4-9.

What followed was a 24-17 upset (in Dallas!) in which the Redskins were able to keep Aikman, Smith, and Irvin under wraps while somehow scoring enough points to overcome a tough Cowboys defense.

Another defeat that would be shrugged off by the losing team and would later result in a Super Bowl down the line, it still doesn't change the fact that when people say "any given Sunday" they mean it! You should never count out your opponent until the game is completed.

CONCLUSION

This brings us to the end of our journey together. I hope you enjoyed the book and had some fun learning about the vibrant history of NFL football to go along with a few inspiring stories and fun facts about the game that I and so many other people love dearly.

I think what I wanted to convey the most through this book is that football gets an unfair reputation. While it is undoubtedly a violent sport that results in injuries to many, this is not enough to write it off as a simply violent game played by violent people.

From the stories of Tom Brady to Doug Baldwin to Michael Oher, I was hoping to convey that these are people, much like us. People who worked incredibly hard to get where they got to.

Football was invented in the late 19th century because there was something about this idea, this idea of combining rugby and soccer into a fully American game that stuck with the general population. While baseball is America's pastime, football is America in its purest form: We are tough, resilient, physical, and love our teammates. This is football, this is what we were brought up learning, and this is what I hope you all can take away from this book.

Moreover, I hope you were able to gain more knowledge about the sport. While the basis of football is quite simple in ideology, the truth of the matter is that there are a ton of different aspects that go into your average football team. Whether you are a coach, viewer, special teams player, offensive player, or defensive player, football is a team sport: plain and simple. You cannot have a weak link if you hope to make it in the NFL. One weak link turns into multiple weak links which turn into a bad football team.

While I don't expect someone who knew nothing about the game to now be an expert about the sport, I do hope that you have a greater appreciation of how much time, effort, and rules go into football. This is not a game for dummies, but rather a game of geniuses trying to outsmart one another!

At the beginning of the book, I spelled out a scenario in which you were watching a football game and were completely lost as to what was happening on your screen. I hope the next time you are watching a game you are not only following along with what is happening but maybe even giving pointers to your friends and family!

If all else fails, don't forget about the fun facts...they were made to impress.

Thank you so much for taking the time to read this book, and if you enjoyed it, please leave a review on Amazon. I appreciate all of you greatly, and I hope you had as much fun reading this book as I did writing it!

References

Alder, J. (2019). *How to Explain Football to Someone Who Has No Clue*. LiveAbout.
https://www.liveabout.com/football-101-the-basics-of-football-1333784

Barrabi, T. (2018, December 6). *XFL, USFL, other pro football leagues that took on the NFL*. FOXBusiness.
https://www.foxbusiness.com/sports/xfl-usfl-aaf-nfl-pro-football-startups

bbcsports. (2015). *BBC Sport - American Football - NFL in a nutshell*. Bbc.co.uk.
http://news.bbc.co.uk/sport2/hi/other_sports/american_football/3192002.stm

Carew, C. (2021, March 1). *Doug Baldwin Jr*. Insightful Player.
https://www.theinsightfulplayer.com/post/doug-baldwin-jr

Daughters, A. (2013, May 17). *The Evolution of Football Equipment*. Bleacher Report; Bleacher Report.
https://bleacherreport.com/articles/1642538-the-evolution-of-football-equipment

Fadullon, J. (2021, May 8). *Updating And Ranking The 50 Greatest NFL Players Of All-Time*. ClutchPoints.
https://clutchpoints.com/updating-and-ranking-the-50-greatest-nfl-players-of-all-time/

Guinness World Records News. (2012, September 4). *10 Guinness World Records to kickoff football season*. Guinness World Records.
https://www.guinnessworldrecords.com/news/2012/9/10-guinness-world-records-to-kickoff-

football-season-
44578/?fb_comment_id=279576182143505_9953
44017233381

http://www.facebook.com/thechrischase. (2015,
October). *101 amazing NFL facts that will blow your
mind*. For the Win; For The Win.
https://ftw.usatoday.com/2015/10/101-amazing-
nfl-facts-that-will-blow-your-mind

NFL Operations. (2019). *Evolution of the NFL Rules | NFL
Football Operations*. Nfl.com.
https://operations.nfl.com/the-rules/evolution-
of-the-nfl-rules/

NFL Throwback. (2019). How EVERY Team Got Its
Name & Identity! [YouTube Video]. In *YouTube*.
https://www.youtube.com/watch?v=ovdbrdCIP7
U

nfl.com. (n.d.). *NFL's most unbreakable records*. NFL.com.
Retrieved November 4, 2021, from
https://www.nfl.com/photos/nfl-s-most-
unbreakable-records-0ap3000000415162

October 20, C. M., & 2021. (2021, October 20). *Which
NFL Team Has The Most Super Bowl Wins?*
Www.one37pm.com.
https://www.one37pm.com/strength/sports/whi
ch-nfl-team-has-the-most-super-bowl-winss

Pro Football Hall of Fame. (2017). *Birth of Pro Football | Pro
Football Hall of Fame Official Site*.
Profootballhof.com.
https://www.profootballhof.com/football-
history/birth-of-pro-football/

Raynolds, J. (2020, October 9). *Starting an NFL Career: Three
inspirational stories to learn from*. Pro Football
Network.
https://www.profootballnetwork.com/starting-

an-nfl-career-three-inspirational-stories-to-learn-from/

Santorsa, T. (2012, May 1). *Ranking the 50 Best NFL Head Coaches of All Time*. Bleacher Report. https://bleacherreport.com/articles/1168549-ranking-the-50-best-nfl-head-coaches-of-all-time

Tallent, A. (2016). *25 Greatest Head Coaches in NFL History*. AthlonSports.com. https://athlonsports.com/nfl/25-greatest-head-coaches-nfl-history

Tallent, A., 3/5/20, & Est, 11:00 A. (2020, March 5). *Ranking the 10 Professional Football Leagues to Compete with the NFL*. AthlonSports.com. https://athlonsports.com/xfl/ranking-10-football-leagues-compete-nfl

topendsports. (n.d.). *American Football basic rules*. Www.topendsports.com. https://www.topendsports.com/sport/gridiron/basics.htm

USA Today Sports. (2019, October). *Jerry Rice, Tom Brady and Lawrence Taylor top our list of the 100 greatest NFL players of all time*. USA TODAY; USA TODAY. https://www.usatoday.com/story/sports/nfl-100/2019/10/01/nfl-100-best-players-all-time/3785514002/

Werner, B. (2019, September 18). *11 of the biggest underdogs to win NFL games*. Touchdown Wire. https://touchdownwire.usatoday.com/2019/09/18/11-of-the-biggest-underdogs-to-win-nfl-games/

Whalen, B. (2011, October 19). *The Greatest Players in NFL History at Each Position*. Bleacher Report. https://bleacherreport.com/articles/895909-the-greatest-players-in-nfl-history-at-each-position

Wikipedia Contributors. (2019a, March 21). *History of American football*. Wikipedia; Wikimedia Foundation. https://en.wikipedia.org/wiki/History_of_American_football

Wikipedia Contributors. (2019b, March 23). *List of National Football League records (individual)*. Wikipedia; Wikimedia Foundation. https://en.wikipedia.org/wiki/List_of_National_Football_League_records_(individual)

CPSIA information can be obtained
at www.ICGtesting.com
Printed in the USA
BVHW040131240423
662815BV00017B/119